MW01617995

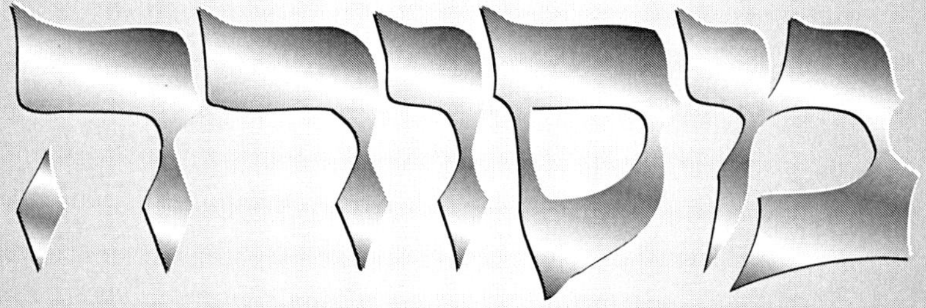

ArtScroll Series®

Rabbi Nosson Scherman / Rabbi Meir Zlotowitz

General Editors

קול דודי על מגילת רות

on Megillas Ruth

COMMENTS, INSIGHTS AND IDEAS
ON THE BOOK OF RUTH
ADAPTED FROM THE SHIURIM OF

RABBI DAVID FEINSTEIN

KOL DODI

Published by
Mesorah Publications, ltd
in conjunction with
MESIVTHA TIFERETH JERUSALEM

FIRST EDITION
First Impression . . . May 2006
Second Impression . . . April 2010
Third Impression . . . March 2021
Fourth Impression . . . February 2023

Published and Distributed by
MESORAH PUBLICATIONS, Ltd.
313 Regina Avenue / Rahway, N.J. 07065

Distributed in Europe by
LEHMANNS
Unit E, Viking Business Park
Rolling Mill Road
Jarrow, Tyne & Wear NE32 3DP
England

Distributed in Australia & New Zealand by
GOLDS WORLD OF JUDAICA
3-13 William Street
Balaclava, Melbourne 3183
Victoria Australia

Distributed in Israel by
SIFRIATI / A. GITLER _ BOOKS
POB 2351
Bnei Brak 51122

Distributed in South Africa by
KOLLEL BOOKSHOP
Northfield Centre, 17 Northfield Avenue
Glenhazel 2192, Johannesburg, South Africa

THE ARTSCROLL JUDAICA CLASSICS®
KOL DODI ON MEGILLAS RUTH

ITEM CODE: KORH
ISBN 10: 1-4226-0046-7
ISBN 13: 978-1-4226-0046-7

Typography by CompuScribe at ArtScroll Studios, Ltd.
313 Regina Avenue / Rahway, N.J. 07065/ (718) 921-9000
Printed in the United States of America
Bound by Sefercraft Inc., Quality Bookbinders, Rahway, NJ

Acknowledgments

A lesson we will see as we study the Book of Ruth is how one should react to favors one receives from a fellow human being. Of course one should thank the person who rendered the service — that is obvious — but it fails to recognize the full truth. One must realize that ultimately the Source of all blessings is Hashem. It is not nearly enough to thank the agent, one must thank the Giver of all good.

It is human nature to thank the agent and not realize that there was a Giver. In the adage of the Sages (*Bava Kamma* 92b), חַמְרָא לְמָרֵיהּ טִיבוּתָא לְשָׁקְיֵיהּ, *The wine belongs to the king, but thanks are given to the waiter* [instead of to the master]. In the Book of Ruth (2:20), we see that Naomi, who was a great lady, *did* recognize the truth. When Ruth informed Naomi that the man who had been kind to her was Boaz, Naomi thanked Hashem for His kindness in bringing them together.

Certainly one must pray that those who become his friends should be good people and that one should not come into the company of bad people. One should realize that nothing is coincidental. Everything is in the hands of the Creator, and if one has had the good fortune to have friends of high caliber, one has been the beneficiary of Hashem's kindness and should thank Him. As we find in *Yalkut Shimoni* (*Tehillim* 740), one should thank Hashem for giving him friends who advise him wisely, rather than friends whose bad advice can cause his downfall.

It is in this spirit that I thank Hashem for blessing me with the good friends who have helped bring this *sefer* to fruition. Foremost among them are the principals of ArtScroll/Mesorah, **RABBI MEIR ZLOTOWITZ**, **RABBI NOSSON SCHERMAN**, and **RABBI SHEAH BRANDER.** I am grateful to the ArtScroll staff who contributed their time, diligence, and expertise to this project. I am grateful to the members of the ArtScroll/Mesorah staff who participated in producing this volume. Avrohom Biderman who read and commented on the manuscript; Moishe Deutsch, Mordechai Guttman, and Sara Rivka Spira who typset and corrected the book; Mrs. Faygie Weibaum who proofread, and Mendy Herzberg, who coordinated all their efforts.

I am grateful to my close friend **R' SHIMON KWESTEL**, who read the manuscript carefully and assisted in the editing.

May this *sefer* add *yiras Shamayim* in the world through the vehicle of Torah study. It was completed just before Purim, the day when the Jewish people accepted the Torah anew with great joy, and it will be published before Shavuos, the day when Hashem gave us the Torah. In the merit of Torah and our people's joyous acceptance of Hashem's word, may we all merit to carry out His will and earn His blessings.

Rabbi David Feinstein
Purim 5766

קול דודי על מגילת רות

KOL DODI
ON MEGILLAS RUTH

Introduction

◈ The Connection to Shavuos

וְנוֹהֲגִים לוֹמַר רוּת בְּשָׁבוּעוֹת

It is customary to read the Book of Ruth on Shavuos (*Rama, Orach Chaim* 490:9)

The festival of Shavuos is nowhere mentioned in the Book of Ruth, nevertheless there are several reasons for the custom to read Ruth on the festival, as follows:

1. The Torah is called תּוֹרַת חֶסֶד, *the Teaching of Kindness,* and the Book of Ruth revolves around lessons about acts and attitudes of kindness. It is therefore appropriate that the festival and the Book should be associated with one another.

2. Immediately after giving the laws of Shavuos (*Leviticus* 23:15-21), the Torah gives the commandment that farmers must leave parts of their harvest in the field, and permit the poor to glean there (ibid. v. 22). This commandment is a central feature of the Book, for it is only because Ruth was gleaning in Boaz's field that she came to meet him, marry him, and thereby become the ancestress of the Davidic dynasty.

   The fact that the Torah teaches the laws of מַתְּנוֹת עֲנִיִּים, *gifts to the poor,* in proximity to Shavuos indicates that there is a connection between the two. When the Jewish people received the Torah, they became "converts to Judaism," as it were, and Judaism requires that one be kind and generous, especially to the poor and the helpless, an attribute that was foreign to most other cultures. In fact, this principle is so basic, one of the questions asked to candidates for conversion is, "Do you accept the laws of giving to the poor?" (*Yevamos* 46b). That is why the Jewish nation was given these laws in conjunction with its becoming God's people.

3. *What is the connection between the Book of Ruth and Shavuos that it is read at the time when the Torah was given? To teach you that the Torah was given only through suffering and poverty* (*Yalkut Shimoni, Ruth* §591). The Midrash means to teach that one cannot expect to become a Torah scholar if he wants to live a life of luxury. On the verse that gives the laws of ritual purity if someone dies in a tent (*Numbers* 19:14), the Sages comment homiletically that *tent* is a metaphor for the study hall, and אֵין אָדָם נַעֲשֶׂה תַּלְמִיד חָכָם עַד שֶׁמֵּמִית עַצְמוֹ עָלֶיהָ, *A person cannot become a Torah scholar unless he "kills himself" [i.e., is prepared to accept privation] for its sake* (*Shabbos* 83b). So, too, a convert who wishes to accept the Torah by becoming a Jew may not do so in order to become rich. The motivation of a person who stands to gain financially by converting is suspect; in fact, during the reign of David and Solomon, when Israel was powerful and wealthy, the courts did not accept converts (*Yevamos* 24b).

   Ruth converted to Judaism although she knew — and Naomi warned her — that she could expect to be poor and not find a husband. Despite this, Ruth insisted on joining the Jewish people. Her name alludes to this choice. The numerical value of her name, רות, is 606. In addition to the seven Noachide laws in which she was already obligated, she chose to accept 606 more, obligating herself in all the 613 commandments of the Torah.

4. Shavuos is the appropriate time to read the Book of Ruth because it contains the genealogy of King David, who was born on Shavuos (*Shaarei Teshuvah, Orach Chaim* 494:2). Parenthetically, he also died on Shavuos (*Yerushalmi, Beitzah* 2:4). The reason for the reason, however, is not merely because of the confluence of dates. In Judaism, the king is God's "executive officer," as it were, as Scripture says when Solomon became king: וַיֵּשֶׁב שְׁלֹמֹה עַל־כִּסֵּא ה׳, *And Solomon sat on the throne of HASHEM* (*I Divrei Hayamim* 29:23). Since the Torah was given on Shavuos, it was appropriate that the king who led the people in studying and observing it should be born on that day.

א/א א וַיְהִי בִּימֵי שְׁפֹט הַשֹּׁפְטִים וַיְהִי רָעָב בָּאָרֶץ וַיֵּלֶךְ אִישׁ מִבֵּית לֶחֶם יְהוּדָה לָגוּר

רש"י

א (א) ויהי בימי שפוט השופטים. לפני מלוך מלך שאול, שהיו הדורות מתפרנסים על ידי שופטים. ובימי אבצן היה, שאמרו רבותינו אבצן זה בועז: וילך איש. עשיר גדול היה ופרנס הדור ויצא מארץ ישראל לחוצה לארץ מפני צרות העין, שהיתה עינו צרה בעניים הבאים לדוחקו, לכך נענש:

Chapter 1

1. **וַיְהִי בִּימֵי שְׁפֹט הַשֹּׁפְטִים** — *And it happened in the days when the Judges judged.*

The Sages teach that use of the word וַיְהִי, *and it was* — instead of the word וְהָיָה, which has the same meaning — indicates that the event being introduced was sad, or even tragic. In the context of this verse, the sadness refers to fact that — as the Talmud's homiletical rendering of the phrase establishes — these were *the days when [the people] judged the Judges*, i.e., that the people were harshly critical of their Judges. Even if the Judges ruled correctly and were justified in admonishing the people for their shortcomings, the public would not accept the rulings and criticism because the Judges were guilty of the same misdeeds. This is a truly tragic situation because when there is an absence of law and order, "a person can swallow his fellow alive" (*Avos* 3:2).

We may add that the use of the verb form שְׁפֹט indicates that public criticism of the Judges was constant. For example, when a person finds a nest of birds, the Torah does not permit him to take the chicks while the mother bird is present. Rather the Torah commands him send away the mother bird. The obligation is phrased in the verb form of שַׁלֵּחַ, to teach that the obligation to send off the mother is constant, and one must do so even a hundred times if the mother bird keeps coming back. Accordingly, in our verse, the implication is that criticism of the Judges went on and on. Consequently, since there was so little respect for the Judges, respect for the law itself broke down.

☐ **וַיְהִי רָעָב בָּאָרֶץ** — *There was a famine in the land.*

This was a natural consequence of the prevalent dishonesty, for, as

1/1 [1] *It happened in the days when the Judges judged, that there was a famine in the land, and a man went from Bethlehem in Judah to sojourn*

---

the Sages teach (*Shabbos* 32b), בַּעֲוֹן גָּזֵל הָרָעָב הֹוֶה, *because of the sin of robbery, famine results.*

Why is famine an appropriate punishment for robbery?

Whatever a person will earn is decided by God, so there is really no reason to steal; if one is entitled to the possessions, he will obtain them legally, and if not, all his machinations will not avail him in the end. By stealing, a person audaciously tells God, in effect, "I do not need You to support me, I have my own ways to make money." God responds, "We will see how successful you will be. Instead of having prosperity, you will have a famine!" As the Sages say (*Sotah* 9a), if someone tries to get what belongs to someone else, he will lose even his own possessions.

☐ **וַיֵּלֶךְ אִישׁ** — *And a man went.*

The term אִישׁ, *a man*, implies that the person in question was great and respected. For example, the Kohanim addressed the Kohen Gadol as אִישִׁי כֹּהֵן גָּדוֹל, *My* **man**, *O High Priest* (*Yoma* 18a). This great man deserted his city because he despaired of finding a way to provide sufficient food for the populace in the face of the famine. In his modesty he felt that he could not exercise leadership in the tragic situation, but he had no right to abdicate his responsibility to the community. Since, as Scripture testifies, he was an אִישׁ, a distinguished man, he could have influenced his peers to contribute money and stores of grain to alleviate the hunger of the needy. Similarly, the righteous people in the generation of the destruction of the First Temple were convinced that their protests against the sinners would be useless, and therefore they remained silent. For that failure they were condemned.

☐ **לָגוּר** — *To sojourn.*

The term לָגוּר, *to sojourn*, indicates a temporary residence, as we say in the Pesach Haggadah that Jacob and his family went to *sojourn in Egypt*, meaning that they had no intention of remaining there permanently. Here, too, Elimelech expected to live in Moab only until the famine ended, whereupon he would return home.

בִּשְׂדֵי מוֹאָב הוּא וְאִשְׁתּוֹ וּשְׁנֵי בָנָיו:
ב וְשֵׁם הָאִישׁ אֱלִימֶלֶךְ וְשֵׁם אִשְׁתּוֹ נָעֳמִי וְשֵׁם
שְׁנֵי־בָנָיו ׀ מַחְלוֹן וְכִלְיוֹן אֶפְרָתִים מִבֵּית
לֶחֶם יְהוּדָה וַיָּבֹאוּ שְׂדֵי־מוֹאָב וַיִּהְיוּ־שָׁם:

רש"י

(ב) אפרתים. חשובים וכן (שמואל-א א, א) בן תוחו בן צוף אפרתי, אבגינו"ס. ראה חשיבותם, שהרי השיא עגלון מלך מואב את בתו למחלון דאמר מר רות בתו של עגלון היתה. ד"א אפרתים, בית לחם קרויה אפרת (בראשית מח, ז):

☐ **בִּשְׂדֵי מוֹאָב** — *In the fields of Moab.*

Although Elimelech left *Eretz Yisrael*, he did not desert the values of Judaism. He chose to sojourn in the rural areas, the *fields*, where he would not be witness to the thievery and immorality that were likely common in the cities.

☐ **הוּא וְאִשְׁתּוֹ** — *He and his wife.*

Elimelech went of his own volition, but Naomi went because she was his wife, so she had no choice but to accompany her husband.

☐ **וּשְׁנֵי בָנָיו** — *And his two sons.*

The verse calls them *his* sons, not *their* sons, implying that Elimelech was the decision-maker of the family. The young men went because their father made the decision and they could not dispute him. After coming to Moab, however, they were influenced by their father's attitude and stayed there even after his passing.

2. **וְשֵׁם הָאִישׁ** — *The man's name.*

Rather than simply identifying the man, Scripture introduces the word שֵׁם, *name*. In Scriptural parlance, this word implies that we are being told not merely *who* the person is, but also *what* he is — his values and his mission. Thus, we must analyze the names to learn what they represent.

☐ **אֱלִימֶלֶךְ** — *Elimelech.*

The word can be translated *to the king*. Elimelech was a descendant of Judah, the tribe of kingship, and he should have been part of the line that would produce King David. It should not have been necessary for the Davidic line to come about through *yibum*, or levirate marriage, as recounted later in this Book, when Boaz married Ruth. Had Elimelech

1/ 2 *in the fields of Moab, he and his wife, and his two sons.*
²The man's name was Elimelech, the name of his
wife Naomi, and the name of his two sons Machlon
and Kilion, Ephrathites of Bethlehem in Judah. They
came to the field of Moab and there they remained.

---

not sinned, he would have been the ancestor of David *the king*, as his name implies, and not merely the vehicle whose actions brought Ruth to the Jewish people, where she was married to Boaz, the union from which David descended.

☐ נָעֳמִי — *Naomi.*

The name means *the pleasant one.* She was not at fault for deserting the hungry people of Judah. She joined her husband because she was *pleasant* and did not wish to cause conflict in the family. Therefore she was not punished when her husband and sons lost their lives in punishment for their selfishness.

☐ מַחְלוֹן — *Machlon.*

The word is related to חוּלִין, *profane* or *mundane.* Machlon profaned himself by marrying a Moabite woman, who had not converted to Judaism. The Sages teach that Abraham rescues his circumcised descendants from Gehinnom, but not if they are married to gentiles. In a sense, Machlon sinned needlessly because, as the further narrative shows, his wife Ruth would have converted and he could have married her in accordance with the Halachah.

☐ וְכִלְיוֹן — *And Kilion.*

The name is related to כְּלָיָה, *destruction.* Kilion was destroyed. Not merely did he die, but his wife Orpah did not convert and marry a Jewish man, so that Kilion never had Jewish posterity, as Machlon would later vicariously have through Ruth.

☐ אֶפְרָתִים — *Ephrathites.*

I.e., from the family of Moses' sister Miriam, who was also known as *Ephrath,* who was an ancestress of the Davidic line. She and her mother were the midwives who had saved the Jewish babies in Egypt from Pharaoh's decree that they be drowned. As their reward, God blessed them with בָּתִּים, *houses* of Kohanim, Levites, and kings (*Sotah* 11b).

☐ וַיִּהְיוּ־שָׁם — *And there they remained.*

This expression is often interpreted to mean that the status quo

ג וַיָּמָת אֱלִימֶלֶךְ אִישׁ נָעֳמִי וַתִּשָּׁאֵר הִיא
ד וּשְׁנֵי בָנֶיהָ: וַיִּשְׂאוּ לָהֶם נָשִׁים מֹאֲבִיּוֹת
שֵׁם הָאַחַת עָרְפָּה וְשֵׁם הַשֵּׁנִית רוּת וַיֵּשְׁבוּ

רש"י

(ג) איש נעמי. למה נאמר, מכאן אמרו (סנהדרין כב, ב) אין איש מת אלא לאשתו. ואמר איש נעמי, כלומר לפי שהוא היה איש נעמי ושולט עליה והיא טפלה לו, לכך פגעה בו מדת הדין ולא בה:

---

remained intact. In this context it would mean that as long as Elimelech was alive, his sons did not marry Moabite women, although after he died they took wives who had not converted to Judaism.

3. אִישׁ נָעֳמִי — *Naomi's husband.*

Before he fled from the famine, he was an אִישׁ, a distinguished citizen and leader of Bethlehem. Now he was merely the husband of Naomi. He had lost his communal status; if he had returned to Bethlehem, the community would not have restored him to his position of leadership. When God created Chavah, the first woman, Adam called her אִשָּׁה; she was a part of him, his wife. Having lost her husband, Naomi was now bereft of that role of אִשָּׁה.

☐ **הִיא וּשְׁנֵי בָנֶיהָ** — *She with her two sons.*

No longer was she a wife who assists and attempts to guide her husband. Now she was a mother, who devoted herself to her children. Without a husband, Naomi was now completely devoted to the other role of Chavah, who was so named because, as Adam explained, she would be אֵם כָּל חָי, *the mother of all human life.*

As the mother of her sons, she felt it was her duty to remain in Moab because Machlon and Kilion did not wish to return to *Eretz Yisrael.*

4. וַיִּשְׂאוּ לָהֶם נָשִׁים מֹאֲבִיּוֹת — *They married for themselves Moabite women.*

Once they decided to remain in Moab, it was necessary for them to wed, because a man needs a wife. As Hashem said after He created Adam, לֹא טוֹב הֱיוֹת הָאָדָם לְבַדּוֹ אֶעֱשֶׂה לּוֹ עֵזֶר כְּנֶגְדּוֹ, *It is not good that man be alone; I will make him a helper corresponding to him* (*Bereishis* 2:18). It is essential to *him*, i.e., to the very essence of a man, that he have a wife, because, as the Sages put it, a man without a mate is not a complete man. This is implied by our verse's use of the word לָהֶם, *for themselves*, i.e., they had to

[3] Elimelech, Naomi's husband, died; and she was
left with her two sons. [4] They married for themselves
Moabite women, the name of the one was Orpah,
and the name of the second one Ruth, and they lived

---

have wives to complete themselves as men. This is why Machlon and Kilion felt compelled to marry, and because there were no Jewish women in Moab, they rationalized that they had to marry Moabite women. This logic was fundamentally flawed, however, since their mating with non-Jewish women did not constitute a legal marriage, and a marriage without halachic standing could not make them "complete." True, they needed wives, but for that they should have returned to *Eretz Yisrael.*

☐ **הָאַחַת** — *The one.*

The word can also be understood as the *only one.* Orpah thought only about herself. When Naomi said that she had no more sons for Orpah to marry and urged her to return to her family, Orpah gave no thought to converting and going to Bethlehem with her mother-in-law. She thought only of herself and remained in Moab.

☐ **עָרְפָּה** — *Orpah.*

The word is related to עֹרֶף, *back.* Orpah was kind and had intended to return with her mother-in-law to *Eretz Yisrael.* But when she was confronted with the fact that it would be difficult for her to marry a Jew even if she converted (see v. 6), she turned her *back* on her plan to stay with Naomi, and she refused to go to *Eretz Yisrael.*

☐ **וְשֵׁם הַשֵּׁנִית** — *And the name of the second one.*

Ruth was willing to attach herself and make herself subordinate to others. She wanted to benefit from the wisdom and guidance of other people. Her descendant King David also subordinated himself to the will of God.

☐ **רוּת** — *Ruth.*

Her name alludes to her descendant, King David, of whom the Sages say: שֶׁרִוָּהוּ לְהקב״ה בְּשִׁירוֹת וְתִשְׁבָּחוֹת, *that He satiated the Holy One, Blessed is He, with songs and praises.* The word רוּת is similar to רִוָּהוּ.

☐ **וַיֵּשְׁבוּ שָׁם** — *They lived there.*

The verse does not say they *sojourned* there, as in verse 1. Now they

ה שָׁם כְּעֶשֶׂר שָׁנִים׃ וַיָּמֻתוּ גַם־שְׁנֵיהֶם מַחְלוֹן
וְכִלְיוֹן וַתִּשָּׁאֵר הָאִשָּׁה מִשְּׁנֵי יְלָדֶיהָ
ו וּמֵאִישָׁהּ׃ וַתָּקָם הִיא וְכַלֹּתֶיהָ וַתָּשָׁב
מִשְּׂדֵי מוֹאָב כִּי שָׁמְעָה בִּשְׂדֵה מוֹאָב
כִּי־פָקַד יהוה אֶת־עַמּוֹ לָתֵת לָהֶם לָחֶם׃
ז וַתֵּצֵא מִן־הַמָּקוֹם אֲשֶׁר הָיְתָה־שָׁמָּה

רש"י

(ה) **גם שניהם.** מהו גם, בתחלה לקו בממונם, ומתו גמליהם ומקניהם, אח"כ מתו גם הם: (ז) **ותצא מן המקום.** למה נאמר, הרי כבר נאמר ותשב משדה מואב ומהיכן תשוב אם לא תצא מן המקום שהיתה שם, אלא מגיד שיציאת צדיק מן המקום ניכרת ועושה רושם, פנה זיוה, פנה הדרה, פנה שבחה של עיר, וכן (בראשית כח, י) ויצא יעקב מבאר שבע:

---

had settled down in Moab and decided to live there permanently.

☐ **כְּעֶשֶׂר שָׁנִים** — *About ten years.*

When Elimelech and the family left the Land, the reigning Judge was Yiftach (see *Shoftim* 11:26). When Naomi and Ruth returned to *Eretz Yisrael*, the judge was Boaz, who, in the Book of Judges, is referred to as Ivtzan. He served until 309 years after Israel entered the Land.

5. וַיָּמֻתוּ — *[Machlon and Kilion] died.*

The juxtaposition of this verse with the previous one, which tells of their marriage to Moabite women, indicates that their death was in punishment for the marriage.

☐ **גַם** — *Also.*

This word always implies something in addition to what is explicitly stated. In this case, Naomi lost not only her family, but also her fortune. As the Sages teach, when Hashem exacts judgment from a person, He begins with lesser penalties — taking away possessions — and if that does not inspire the person to repent, He extends the punishment to health and life.

☐ **וַתִּשָּׁאֵר הָאִשָּׁה** — *The woman was bereft.*

Now she was totally alone, without her husband, her children, or her property in Bethlehem. (Since the wives of her sons were not Jewish, their marriages were not halachically valid, so she did not even have

1/5-7

there about ten years. [5] *The two of them, Machlon and Kilion, also died; and the woman was bereft of her two children and of her husband.*

[6] *She then arose along with her daughters-in-law and she returned from the fields of Moab, for she had heard in the fields of Moab that HASHEM had remembered His people by giving them food.* [7] *She left the place where she had been,*

---

daughters-in-law.)

Having lost her husband, she was no longer a wife. Having lost her children, she was no longer a mother. Utterly alone, she was like a child and resolved to go back to בֵּית אָבִיהָ, *her ancestral home.*

6. וַתָּקָם — *She then arose.*

This term indicates moving in a new direction. All three women were embarking upon great changes in their lives, and Scripture uses the singular form, because each of them had her own motive, as follows:

☐ **הִיא** — *She,*

i.e., Naomi, who was leaving Moab to return home.

☐ **וְכַלֹּתֶיהָ** — *With her daughters-in-law.*

At first, Ruth and Orpah accompanied Naomi with the intention of remaining *her daughters-in-law,* by going to Bethlehem with her and converting to Judaism.

☐ **וַתָּשָׁב** — *And she returned.*

The verb is in the singular, because Naomi planned to return home alone, since she would advise the two young women to go back to their families. Alternatively, only she could be said to *return,* since she was going back home. Her daughters-in-law, however, had never converted and had never been in *Eretz Yisrael,* so even if they had decided to go with her, they could not be said to "return."

☐ **כִּי־פָקַד ה׳ אֶת־עַמּוֹ לָתֵת לָהֶם לָחֶם** — *That HASHEM had remembered His people by giving them food.* Since God had ended the famine, there would be enough food for her, a destitute widow, as well.

7. וַתֵּצֵא מִן־הַמָּקוֹם — *She left the place.*

As the Sages say on the similar verse, which tells of Jacob's de-

א / ח וּשְׁתֵּי כַלֹּתֶיהָ עִמָּהּ וַתֵּלַכְנָה בַדֶּרֶךְ לָשׁוּב אֶל־
ח אֶרֶץ יְהוּדָה׃ וַתֹּאמֶר נָעֳמִי לִשְׁתֵּי כַלֹּתֶיהָ לֵכְנָה
°יַעַשׂ ק שֹּׁבְנָה אִשָּׁה לְבֵית אִמָּהּ °יעשה יְהוָה עִמָּכֶם
חֶסֶד כַּאֲשֶׁר עֲשִׂיתֶם עִם־הַמֵּתִים וְעִמָּדִי׃

---

parture from Beer-sheva (*Bereishis* 20:10), "A righteous person's departure from a place leaves a void. As long as such a person lives in a city, he constitutes its glory, its splendor, and its beauty; when he departs, its glory, splendor, and beauty depart with him." The same applies to Naomi. When she left Moab, the place lost its spiritual glory, beauty, and splendor.

☐ **וּשְׁתֵּי כַלֹּתֶיהָ עִמָּהּ** — *Her two daughters-in-law with her.*
The beginning of the verse implies that Naomi was the primary person *leaving* Moab. The two women went along to escort her. In the end, only Ruth stayed with her to convert and hope to find a Jewish husband.

☐ **וַתֵּלַכְנָה בַדֶּרֶךְ** — *They set out on the road,*
i.e., the road that led directly to the land of Judah. At first all three women were on the same road, to go to Judah, not only Naomi but also both young women. The verse refers to them as Naomi's daughters-in-law, even though their husbands had died, because they wanted to convert and continue along the way with her to the land of Judah. Had they done so and converted to Judaism, they would remain connected to her as if they were her legal daughters-in-law.

8. לִשְׁתֵּי כַלֹּתֶיהָ — *To her two daughters-in-law.*
The word שְׁתֵּי, *two*, appears to be unnecessary. It indicates that the two were equal, as in the service of Yom Kippur, of which the Torah states that there should be שְׁנֵי הַשְּׂעִירִם, *two he-goats* (*Vayikra* 16:7). The Sages teach that this word means that the two animals should be similar in appearance, height, and value (*Yoma* 62b). In our verse also, the word implies that Naomi considered the two widows to be equal. In fact, both Orpah and Ruth were kind and dedicated. Naomi did not expect Ruth to show such a totally extraordinary degree of loyalty and idealism.

☐ **לֵכְנָה שֹּׁבְנָה** — *Go, return.*
Do not continue with me on the road to Bethlehem; turn around and go on the road to your mothers' homes.

her two daughters-in-law with her, and they set
out on the road to return to the land of Judah.
8 *Then Naomi said to her two daughters-in-*
law, "Go, return, each of you to her mother's
house. May Hashem do kindness with you, as
you did with the dead and with me!

☐ לְבֵית אִמָּהּ — *To her mother's house.*

Tamar, the widow of Judah's sons, was told to return to her *father's* house (*Bereishis* 38:11). Why does this verse speak of their mothers' homes? The women of Moab were modest, while the men were promiscuous, like their forefather Lot. Naomi intimated to them that they should emulate their mothers, not their fathers.

☐ יַעַשׂ ה' — *May* HASHEM *do.*

The word is written in the masculine form, יַעֲשֶׂה, but it is pronounced in the feminine form, without a *hei*, which implies that less strength is needed. Naomi was intimating to them that their kindness to her and their late husbands made them abundantly deserving of God's kindness; there was no need to pray for Him to "exert" Himself, as it were, to show them kindness. They had earned it.

☐ עִמָּכֶם — *With you.*

This word is in the masculine form, which represents strength and not needing the physical help of another; another implication that they were deserving of kindness and had *earned* God's benevolence.

☐ כַּאֲשֶׁר עֲשִׂיתֶם — *As you did.*

Again Scripture uses the masculine form. The two women forgave payment of the *kesubah* (*Midrash Rabbah*),[1] a wife's financial settlement in the event of her husband's death. They behaved like men, who do not receive a payment if they are widowed, because they are regarded as financially self-sufficient.

The daughters of Lot had acted selflessly to ensure the continuation of humanity when they mistakenly thought that they were the only survivors left in the world after the destruction of Sodom. Their de-

---

1. Obviously, Ruth and Orpah forgave payment of the *kesubah* only to the extent that Naomi would benefit, i.e., anything that Ruth collected on her *kesubah* would belong to Naomi.

ט יִתֵּן יְהוָה לָכֶם וּמְצֶאןָ מְנוּחָה אִשָּׁה
בֵּית אִישָׁהּ וַתִּשַּׁק לָהֶן וַתִּשֶּׂאנָה
י קוֹלָן וַתִּבְכֶּינָה׃ וַתֹּאמַרְנָה־לָּהּ כִּי־
יא אִתָּךְ נָשׁוּב לְעַמֵּךְ׃ וַתֹּאמֶר נָעֳמִי שֹׁבְנָה
בְנֹתַי לָמָּה תֵלַכְנָה עִמִּי הַעוֹד־לִי בָנִים
יב בְּמֵעַי וְהָיוּ לָכֶם לַאֲנָשִׁים׃ שֹׁבְנָה בְנֹתַי

---

scendants, Ruth and Orpah, were also selfless in their devotion and kindness.

When the Israelites were marching through the land of Moab on their way to *Eretz Yisrael,* the Moabite men did not greet them with food and water, and they were condemned for that. The women, however, were not blamed because it would have been immodest of them to go out in public with provisions. In using the masculine form, Naomi was intimating here that if Ruth and Orpah would have been alive at that time, and the women had been expected to go out, she was certain that Ruth and Orpah would have brought provisions.

9. לָכֶם — *That you.*

Naomi used the masculine form, as if to say that when they remarry they will be secure enough not to fear that they will be divorced and forced to depend on the kindness of others.

□ **מְנוּחָה** — *Security.*

Your new marriages will not be like the first ones, after which you were forced to return to your mothers. Your second husbands will give you a sense of permanent security.

□ **וַתִּשַּׁק לָהֶן וַתִּשֶּׂאנָה קוֹלָן וַתִּבְכֶּינָה** — *She kissed them, and they raised their voice and wept.*

This was meant to be their final parting from one another. They wept because קָשָׁה עָלַי פְּרֵדַתְכֶם, *It is hard for me to part from you.* Naomi had told them that they must go back to their families because in Moab they would find husbands, but in Judah they would not be able to find Jewish men to marry them.

10. וַתֹּאמַרְנָה־לָּהּ — *And they said to her.*

After they had tearfully bid farewell to one another, the widows had a change of heart and said that they would not leave her; they would go to

[9] *May Hashem grant that you may find security,*
each in the home of her husband." She kissed
them, and they raised their voice and wept. [10] *And*
they said to her, "No, we will return with you to
your people." [11] *But Naomi said, "Turn back, my*
daughters. Why should you come with me? Have I
more sons in my womb who could become
husbands to you? [12] *Turn back, my daughters,*

Bethlehem and convert to Judaism.

☐ כִּי־אִתָּךְ נָשׁוּב ☐ — *We will return with you.*

The word אִתָּךְ, *with you*, implies that they wanted to be Jewish like her and subordinate to her. Indeed, when Ruth had a child, the neighbors said that a baby had been born to Naomi, so much did Ruth and Orpah consider Naomi to be important in their lives.

☐ לְעַמֵּךְ ☐ — *To your people.*

I.e., we will convert to Judaism and become part of *your people.*

11. הַעוֹד־לִי בָנִים בְּמֵעַי — *Have I more sons in my womb?*

Naomi understood that they may be looking forward to marrying Jewish men because they knew from experience that Jews make good husbands, but she tried to dissuade them by giving very down-to-earth advice. By saying that they could marry only if she could give birth to more sons, she alluded to the halachic difficulty that would face them when they sought Jewish mates, as follows:

The Torah states: לֹא־יָבֹא עַמּוֹנִי וּמוֹאָבִי בִּקְהַל ה׳, *An Ammonite or Moabite shall not enter the congregation of God* (*Devarim* 23:4), meaning that although they may convert, they may not marry Jewish women. However, the prohibition applies only to Ammonite and Moabite men, not to women; Jews *are* permitted to marry female converts from these nations (*Yevamos* 76b). Halachically, therefore, Ruth and Orpah could have married Jewish men — but this law was relatively unknown in that time, as we will see later in this Book. Even Doeg, who was one of the nation's leading scholars in the time of King David, did not know it.

Naomi knew the law, so she said that if she had more sons, there would be no problem — but at her age it could not happen, so why should her daughters-in-law subject themselves to hopelessly lonely lives?

א/יג־יד

לֵ֤כְןָ כִּ֥י זָקַ֖נְתִּי מִהְי֣וֹת לְאִ֑ישׁ כִּ֤י אָמַ֙רְתִּי֙
יֶשׁ־לִ֣י תִקְוָ֔ה גַּ֣ם הָיִ֤יתִי הַלַּ֙יְלָה֙ לְאִ֔ישׁ וְגַ֖ם
יג יָלַ֥דְתִּי בָנִֽים׃ הֲלָהֵ֣ן ׀ תְּשַׂבֵּ֗רְנָה עַ֚ד אֲשֶׁ֣ר
יִגְדָּ֔לוּ הֲלָהֵן֙ תֵּֽעָגֵ֔נָה לְבִלְתִּ֖י הֱי֣וֹת לְאִ֑ישׁ
אַ֣ל בְּנֹתַ֗י כִּֽי־מַר־לִ֤י מְאֹד֙ מִכֶּ֔ם כִּֽי־יָצְאָ֥ה
יד בִ֖י יַד־יְהוָֽה׃ יד *וַתִּשֶּׂ֣נָה קוֹלָ֔ן וַתִּבְכֶּ֖ינָה ע֑וֹד
וַתִּשַּׁ֤ק עָרְפָּה֙ לַחֲמוֹתָ֔הּ וְר֖וּת דָּ֥בְקָה בָּֽהּ׃

* חסר א'

רש"י

(יב) **כי זקנתי מהיות לאיש.** שאנשא לו ואוליד בנים ותנשאו להם, שאינם אסורים לכם ואינכם אסורות להם משום אשת אחיו שלא היה בעולמו שאינה זקוקה ליבם, לפי שלא היו למחלון וכליון קדושין בהן, שנכריות היו ולא נתגיירו, ועכשיו הן באות להתגייר, כמו שנאמר כי אתך נשוב לעמך, מעתה נהיה לעם אחד: **כי אמרתי יש לי תקוה.** כי אפילו אמר לי לבי יש לי תקוה לינשא עוד וללדת בנים: **גם הייתי הלילה לאיש.** ויותר מכן, אפילו הריתי הלילה זכרים: **וגם ילדתי בנים.** או אפילו כבר ילדתי בנים: (יג) **הלהן תשברנה.** בתמיה, שמא להם תצפנה עד אשר יגדלו, לשון (תהלים קמו, ה) שברו על ה' אלהיו: **תעגנה.** לשון אסור כלא, כמו (תענית יט, א) עג עוגה ועמד בתוכה. ויש פותרין לשון עיגון ולא יתכן, שאם כן היה לו לינקד הנו"ן דגש או לכתוב שני נוני"ן: **כי יצאה בי יד ה'.** אמר רבי לוי כל מקום שנאמר יד ה' מכת דבר היא, ובנין אב לכולם (שמות ט, ג) הנה יד ה' הויה:

12. לֵכְןָ — *Go along.*

The word is pronounced as if it were spelled with a *hei*, denoting the plural, since she was speaking to both of them. It is spelled without the *hei*, however, to allude to what actually happened: Only Orpah went back to Moab; Ruth went on to *Eretz Yisrael.* The Sages make a similar derivation on verse 9, where the word וּמְצֶאןָ, *you may find,* is spelled without a *hei*, because only Ruth, not Orpah, found a husband in Bethlehem. Even though grammatically the presence or absence of the *hei* does not change the meaning, the allusion is suggested by the fact that the word without the *hei* has fewer letters, as if to say it is a weaker plural.

13. הֲלָהֵן תְּשַׂבֵּרְנָה — *Would you wait for them?*

Since Naomi was speaking about baby boys, the verse should have used the masculine form הֲלָהֶם. Perhaps she meant to allude to the word

1/ 13-14 *go, for I am too old to have a husband. Even if I were to say, 'There is hope for me!' and even if I were to have a husband tonight — and even bear sons —* [13] *would you wait for them until they were grown up? Would you tie yourselves down for them, not to marry anyone else? No, my daughters! I am very embittered on account of you, for the hand of Hashem has gone forth against me."*

[14] *They raised their voice and wept again. Orpah kissed her mother-in-law, but Ruth clung to her.*

הֵן, *yes*, as if to say, "Yes, you may hope that I could present you with male children, but is such a hope rational?"

☐ כִּי־מַר־לִי מְאֹד מִכֶּם — *I am very embittered on account of you.*

I am embittered because I understand very well that you want what every woman desires: חוּטְרָא לְיָדָהּ וּמַקֵּל לִקְבוּרָה, *a staff for her hand and a shovel for burial*, i.e., children who will provide for her in her old age. If a woman has that sense of security, she feels equal to a man, because she is not at a disadvantage — this is the allusion of the word מִכֶּם, *because of you*, in the masculine form. I do not have any more children, so I feel your pain. Therefore, I implore you to go back to Moab and marry.

14. וַתִּבְכֶּינָה עוֹד — *And wept again.*

After Naomi's declaration that the women could not look forward to a future in *Eretz Yisrael*, there was a renewed display of emotion, and they wept again.

☐ וַתִּשַּׁק עָרְפָּה לַחֲמוֹתָהּ — *Orpah kissed her mother-in-law.*

Orpah's kiss was more than a loving farewell to Naomi. She was saying good-bye to Naomi's relationship to her as a mother-in-law. That relationship would now be severed, for Orpah was about to return to Moab to seek a new husband.

☐ וְרוּת דָּבְקָה־בָּהּ — *But Ruth clung to her.*

Ruth wanted Naomi to retain something of their relationship. Indeed, when Ruth bore a child, the infant was regarded as Naomi's son.

א / טו־יז

טו וַתֹּ֗אמֶר הִנֵּה֙ שָׁ֣בָה יְבִמְתֵּ֔ךְ אֶל־עַמָּ֖הּ וְאֶל־
טז אֱלֹהֶ֑יהָ שׁ֖וּבִי אַחֲרֵ֥י יְבִמְתֵּֽךְ׃ וַתֹּ֤אמֶר רוּת֙
אַל־תִּפְגְּעִי־בִ֔י לְעָזְבֵ֖ךְ לָשׁ֣וּב מֵאַחֲרָ֑יִךְ כִּ֠י
אֶל־אֲשֶׁ֨ר תֵּלְכִ֜י אֵלֵ֗ךְ וּבַאֲשֶׁ֤ר תָּלִ֙ינִי֙ אָלִ֔ין
יז עַמֵּ֣ךְ עַמִּ֔י וֵאלֹהַ֖יִךְ אֱלֹהָֽי׃ בַּאֲשֶׁ֤ר תָּמ֙וּתִי֙
אָמ֔וּת וְשָׁ֖ם אֶקָּבֵ֑ר כֹּה֩ יַעֲשֶׂ֨ה יְהוָ֥ה לִי֙ וְכֹ֣ה

רש"י

(טו) **הנה שבה יבמתך.** זה טעמו למעלה תחת השי"ן לפי שהוא לשון עבר, (אסתר ב, יד) ובבקר היא שבה טעמו למטה בבי"ת לפי שהוא לשון הווה, וכן כל כיוצא בהם: (טז) **אל תפגעי בי.** אל תפצרי בי: **כי אל אשר תלכי אלך.** מכאן אמרו רבותינו ז"ל (יבמות מז, א) גר שבא להתגייר מודיעין לו מקצת עונשים שאם בא לחזור, בו יחזור שמתוך דבריה של רות אתה למד מה שאמרה לה נעמי. אסור לנו לצאת חוץ לתחום בשבת, א"ל **באשר תלכי אלך.** אסור לנו להתייחד נקבה עם זכר שאינו אישה, אמרה לה **באשר תליני אלין.** עמנו מובדלים מאחר עמים בשש מאות ושלש עשרה מצות, **עמך עמי.** אסור לנו ע"א, **אלהיך אלהי.** ארבע מיתות נמסרו לבית דין, **באשר תמותי אמות.** שני קברים נמסרו לבית דין, אחד לנסקלין ונשרפין ואחד לנהרגין ונחנקין, אמרה לה **ושם אקבר:** (יז) **כה יעשה ה' לי.** כאשר התחיל להרע שילאה בי ידו להמית אישי ולירד מנכסי:

---

15. **שָׁבָה יְבִמְתֵּךְ** — *Your sister-in law has returned.*

If you go back with her, you may well become sisters-in-law again, for you may marry Moabite brothers, and thus there you will still have a close relationship.

☐ **וְאֶל־אֱלֹהֶיהָ** — *And to her gods.*

Since she is going back to the idols of Moab, it is clear that she does not believe in Hashem. If so, even if she were to find a Jewish mate, "her conversion" would not be valid because she would not be accepting Judaism. Therefore...

☐ **שׁוּבִי אַחֲרֵי יְבִמְתֵּךְ** — *Go follow your sister-in-law.*

Assuming that Ruth, too, had lost faith in Hashem, Naomi meant to say that there was no future for her in *Eretz Yisrael*, for marriage to a Jew would be impossible.

16. **אַל־תִּפְגְּעִי־בִי** — *Do not urge me.*

1/ 15-17 [15] *So she said, "Look, your sister-in-law has*
returned to her people and to her gods; go follow
your sister-in-law." [16] *But Ruth said, "Do not urge*
me to leave you, to turn back from following you.
For where you go, I will go; where you lodge, I will
lodge; your people are my people, and your God is
my God; [17] *where you die, I will die, and there I will*
be buried. Thus may Hashem do to me, and so
may He do more, if anything but death separates

The word פְּגִיעָה also has the connotation of *prayer* (see *Rashi* to *Bereishis* 28:11). Accordingly, Ruth meant to intimate that Naomi should not pray that God should influence her to go back to Moab.

☐ **אֲשֶׁר תֵּלְכִי** — *Where you go,*
to perform a mitzvah.

☐ **וּבַאֲשֶׁר תָּלִינִי** — *Where you lodge,*
i.e., wherever it is permissible to lodge.

☐ **עַמֵּךְ** — *Your people.*
She alluded to the blessing that God put into the mouth of Bilaam: הֶן־עָם לְבָדָד יִשְׁכֹּן, *Behold! it is a nation that will dwell in solitude.* The word בָּדָד has the numerical value of ten, alluding to the Ten Commandments. As many commentators note, the Ten Commandments encompass all 613 commandments — and the only nation on earth that is commanded to observe them all is Israel.

And *your people* observe the precept of תָּמִים תִּהְיֶה עִם ה׳ אֱלֹקֶיךָ, *You shall be wholehearted with* HASHEM, *your God.* This commandment means that every Jew must acknowledge that whatever God gives us is *whole* and *perfect*, and that we lack nothing essential. This is a unique attribute of Israel, and Ruth wanted to become part of such a nation.

17. בַּאֲשֶׁר תָּמוּתִי — *Where you die,*
if you are punished for transgressing the commandments.

☐ **וְשָׁם אֶקָּבֵר** — *And there I will be buried.*
If death comes because of sins, I am ready to be buried in disgrace.

☐ **כֹּה יַעֲשֶׂה ה׳ לִי** — *Thus may* HASHEM *do to me.*
She did not specify what God should do to her, because one should

יח יוֹסִיף כִּי הַמָּוֶת יַפְרִיד בֵּינִי וּבֵינֵךְ: וַתֵּרֶא
כִּי־מִתְאַמֶּצֶת הִיא לָלֶכֶת אִתָּהּ וַתֶּחְדַּל
יט לְדַבֵּר אֵלֶיהָ: וַתֵּלַכְנָה שְׁתֵּיהֶם עַד־בּוֹאָנָה
בֵּית לָחֶם וַיְהִי כְּבוֹאָנָה בֵּית לֶחֶם וַתֵּהֹם
כָּל־הָעִיר עֲלֵיהֶן וַתֹּאמַרְנָה הֲזֹאת נָעֳמִי:
כ וַתֹּאמֶר אֲלֵיהֶן אַל־תִּקְרֶאנָה לִי נָעֳמִי

רש"י

וכה יוסיף. אם יפריד ביני וביניך כי אם המות: **(יח) ותחדל לדבר אליה.** מכאן אמרו (שם מז, ב) אין מרבין עליו ואין מדקדקין עליו: **(יט) ותלכנה שתיהם.** אמר רבי אבהו בא וראה כמה חביבים הגרים לפני הקב"ה, כיון שנתנה דעתה להתגייר השוה אותה הכתוב לנעמי: **ותהם כל העיר.** נעשית הומיה כל העיר, כולם נתקבצו לקבור אשתו של בועז שמתה בו ביום: **הזאת נעמי.** ה"א נקודה חטף מפני שהיא בתמיה, הזאת נעמי שרגילה לצאת בלבים ובפרדים, חזיתם מה עלתה לה על אשר יצאתה לחוצה לארץ:

---

not speak explicitly of bad things. She merely implied that retribution would follow in the wake of sin.

☐ **כִּי הַמָּוֶת יַפְרִיד בֵּינִי וּבֵינֵךְ** — *If anything but death separates me from you.*

So determined was Ruth to go to *Eretz Yisrael* with Naomi that only death could keep them apart. Ruth said that the only thing that could prevent her from going was if she were to die there in Moab.

18. וַתֵּרֶא כִּי־מִתְאַמֶּצֶת הִיא — *When she [Naomi] saw that she [Ruth] was determined.*

Naomi had urged her three times to turn back, but Ruth had refused every time. Three times constitutes a חֲזָקָה, *presumption*. Once it was established that Ruth would refuse all her entreaties, Naomi accepted Ruth's decision as final and stopped trying to dissuade her.

☐ **וַתֶּחְדַּל לְדַבֵּר אֵלֶיהָ** — *She stopped arguing with her.*

The Sages derive from this that there are limits to how much one should try to dissuade a potential convert and also that one should not be too exacting in evaluating the intentions of a convert (*Yevamos* 47b).

1/ 18-20 *me from you."* [18] *When she saw that she was*
determined to go with her, she stopped arguing
with her, [19] *and the two of them went on until they*
came to Bethlehem.
And it came to pass, when they arrived in Beth-
lehem, the entire city was tumultuous over them,
and the women said, "Could this be Naomi?"
[20] *She said to them, "Do not call me Naomi*
[pleasant one], call me Mara [embittered one], for

---

19. שְׁתֵּיהֶם — *The two of them.*

This word implies that Naomi and Ruth went as equals. *Rashi* comments that this was because Ruth had demonstrated that her determination to convert was completely sincere. That being the case, the spiritual status of the two women was the same. Furthermore, they both had as their goal to go to the land of God. The suffix of this word, a *mem*, is a masculine form. They were returning even though they might not find marriage partners, and remain alone and self-sufficient, like men.

☐ וַיְהִי — *And it came to pass.*

As noted above (v. 1), this word implies sadness or distress. As *Rashi* comments, the people of Bethlehem were in mourning because they were burying the wife of their leader, Boaz.

☐ הֲזֹאת נָעֳמִי — *"Could this be Naomi?"*

A name in Scripture denotes a person's destiny. Since she had been named Naomi, which means pleasantness, she was destined to have a pleasant life. Indeed, as *Rashi* notes, the people were astonished because they remembered her as a woman who had always lived luxuriously, but who had lost God's sheltering protection and become a pauper because she had left *Eretz Yisrael.*

20. אֲלֵיהֶן — *To them.*

The word is in the feminine form, because the men and women did not mingle, even during the eulogies for Boaz's wife. Naomi addressed only the women.

☐ קְרֶאןָ לִי מָרָא — *Call me Mara [Embittered One].*

The word *Mara* is spelled with an *aleph*, rather than a *hei*, to allude to

כא קְרֶאןָ לִי֙ מָרָ֔א כִּֽי־הֵמַ֥ר שַׁדַּ֛י לִ֖י מְאֹֽד׃ אֲנִי֙
מְלֵאָ֣ה הָלַ֔כְתִּי וְרֵיקָ֖ם הֱשִׁיבַ֣נִי יְהוָ֑ה לָ֣מָּה
תִקְרֶ֤אנָה לִי֙ נָֽעֳמִ֔י וַֽיהוָה֙ עָ֣נָה בִ֔י וְשַׁדַּ֖י
כב הֵ֥רַע־לִֽי׃ וַתָּ֣שָׁב נָֽעֳמִ֗י וְר֨וּת הַמּוֹאֲבִיָּ֤ה
כַלָּתָהּ֙ עִמָּ֔הּ הַשָּׁ֖בָה מִשְּׂדֵ֣י מוֹאָ֑ב וְהֵ֗מָּה
בָּ֚אוּ בֵּ֣ית לֶ֔חֶם בִּתְחִלַּ֖ת קְצִ֥יר שְׂעֹרִֽים׃

רש"י

(כא) מלאה הלכתי. בעושר ובנים. ד"א שהיתה מעוברת: **ענה בי.** העיד עלי שהרשעתי לפניו. ד"א ענה בי מדת הדין, כמו (הושע ה, ה) וענה גאון ישראל: **(כב) בתחלת קציר שעורים.** בקצירת העומר הכתוב מדבר:

the word מָרָא, *shovel.* Naomi implied that she had very little reason to be called *Pleasant One.* Her future would not be one of happiness, but of the grave. And she would be her own *shovel*, so to speak, because she had no husband or children.

☐ **שַׁדַּי** — *The Almighty.*

The root of this Divine Name is דַּי, *enough* or *sufficient*, meaning that God in His wisdom provides everyone with his Divinely ordained needs. Naomi bemoaned her plight, implying that by going to Moab she sought more than God wanted her to have, and she transgressed the commandment תָּמִים תִּהְיֶה עִם ה׳ אֱלֹקֶיךָ, to be *wholehearted* and accepting of what God gives. And as a result, she lost even what He had given her.

21. אֲנִי מְלֵאָה . . . רֵיקָם — *I [went] full . . . empty.*

I thought that my "fullness" — i.e., my wealth, family, and position — were truly mine, and not God's gift. Because of that, He brought me back here *empty*, with nothing.

☐ **וַה׳ עָנָה בִי** — HASHEM *has testified against me.*

The word עָנָה, *testified*, is similar to עִנּוּי, *suffering.* God inflicted suffering upon me to teach me that nothing is in human hands; His will is supreme.

22. וַתָּשָׁב נָעֳמִי וְרוּת — *And so Naomi returned, and Ruth . . .*

Even though the two of them returned together, the verb is in the

the Almighty has dealt very bitterly with me. [21] *I was full when I went away, but Hashem has brought me back empty. Why shall you call me Naomi; Hashem has testified against me, the Almighty has brought misfortune upon me!"*

[22] *And so Naomi returned, and Ruth the Moabite, her daughter-in-law, with her — who returned from the fields of Moab. They came to Bethlehem at the beginning of the barley harvest.*

---

singular, to show that the primary one who returned was Naomi. Ruth came because she was convinced to do so by Naomi's example.

☐ **כַּלָּתָהּ** — *Her daughter-in-law.*

Since Ruth's marriage to Naomi's son was not halachically valid, she was never truly a daughter-in-law, and now, after having been widowed, she was surely not related to Naomi. Nevertheless her loyalty to Naomi was as powerful as ever, and she treated Naomi as if they were closely related.

☐ **הַשָּׁבָה** — *Who returned.*

The word refers to Ruth, but it seems to be misapplied: Ruth had never been in *Eretz Yisrael* — how could she be said to "return"? Rather the word alludes to her ancestress, Lot's daughter, who was a native of Sodom, which would become part of the territory of Judah. Lot's daughter was destined — through Ruth — to return to the land of Judah. God says: מָצָאתִי דָּוִד עַבְדִּי, *I found David, My servant* (*Tehillim* 89:21), and Lot's daughters are described as הַנִּמְצָאֹת, *who are found* in Sodom (*Bereishis* 19:15). From the similarity of the words, the Sages infer that God discovered David in the destruction of Sodom, when Lot and his daughters were saved (*Yevamos* 77a).

☐ **בִּתְחִלַּת קְצִיר שְׂעֹרִים** — *At the beginning of the barley harvest.*

From this fact, we can tell when Naomi and Ruth arrived. The barley harvest begins when grain is cut for the Omer offering, on the second day of Pesach.

°מוֹדַע ק׳

א וּלְנָעֳמִי °מידע לְאִישָׁהּ אִישׁ גִּבּוֹר חַיִל
ב מִמִּשְׁפַּחַת אֱלִימֶלֶךְ וּשְׁמוֹ בֹּעַז: וַתֹּאמֶר
רוּת הַמּוֹאֲבִיָּה אֶל־נָעֳמִי אֵלְכָה־נָּא
הַשָּׂדֶה וַאֲלַקֳטָה בַשִּׁבֳּלִים אַחַר אֲשֶׁר
אֶמְצָא־חֵן בְּעֵינָיו וַתֹּאמֶר לָהּ לְכִי בִתִּי:
ג וַתֵּלֶךְ וַתָּבוֹא וַתְּלַקֵּט בַּשָּׂדֶה אַחֲרֵי

רש"י

ב (א) **מודע.** קרוב, בן אחיו של אלימלך היה. אמרו רבותינו ז"ל (בבא בתרא צא, א) אלימלך ושלמון אבי בועז ופלוני אלמוני הגואל ואבי נעמי כולם בני נחשון בן עמינדב היו, ולא הועילה להם זכות אבותם בצאתם מהארץ לחוצה לארץ: (ב) **אלכה נא השדה.** לאחד משדות אנשי העיר, אחרי אחד מהם אשר אמצא חן בעיניו שלא יגער בי: **ואלקטה בשבלים אחר אשר אמצא חן בעיניו.** אחר מי אשר אמצא חן בעיניו: (ג) **ותלך ותבוא ותלקט בשדה.** מצינו במדרש רות, עד לא אזלת אתת, שהוא אומר ותבא ואחר ותלקט אלא שהיתה מסמנת הדרכים קודם שנכנסה לשדה, והלכה ובאה וחזרה לעיר כדי לעשות סימנים וציונים שלא תטעה בשבילין ותדע לשוב:

Chapter 2

1. **וּלְנָעֳמִי מוֹדַע לְאִישָׁהּ** — *Naomi had a relative through her husband.*

This man, Boaz, was her relative, as well, but the verse mentions her husband, Elimelech, because the narrative will involve the right of inheritance and the mitzvah of *yibum* (levirate marriage, by means of which a close relative marries a childless widow). Both inheritance and *yibum* go through the husband's family line. Boaz was a son of Elimelech's brother and Naomi was a daughter of another brother, so that Boaz was Elimelech's nephew and Naomi's cousin (*Bava Basra* 91a).

☐ **אִישׁ גִּבּוֹר חַיִל** — *A man of substance.*

The term implies someone who was skilled and successful at what he did. The numerical value of חַיִל is forty-eight. Since Boaz was the Judge of the nation, he was an outstanding Torah scholar, and the Sages teach that there are forty-eight ways to acquire Torah knowledge (*Avos* 6:5).

☐ **וּשְׁמוֹ בֹּעַז** — *Whose name was Boaz.*

The name is a contraction of the two words: בּוֹ עֹז, *In him is strength.* The letters of his name can be rearranged to spell עָזַב, *forsaken,* but, as Naomi exclaimed below (v. 20) after learning that Boaz had been kind

[1] *Naomi had a relative through her husband, a man of substance, from the family of Elimelech; his name was Boaz.*

[2] *Ruth the Moabite said to Naomi, "Let me go out to the field and I will glean among the ears of grain after I find favor in someone's eyes."*

She said to her, "Go, my daughter." [3] *So she went and came and gleaned in the field behind*

---

to Ruth, *"Blessed is he . . .* אֲשֶׁר לֹא־עָזַב חַסְדּוֹ, *for not failing in his kindness,"* since Boaz had not forsaken her.

2. הַמּוֹאֲבִיָּה — *The Moabite.*

In proposing to Naomi that she would go out to the fields to try and gather kernels of grain, one might have feared that Ruth was taking an unacceptable risk that ordinary field hands might try to socialize with her improperly. In response to this fear, the verse describes her as a Moabite, and since most people still thought that even a Moabite woman was forbidden to Israelites, there was no reason for her to be afraid.

☐ **וַאֲלַקֳטָה בַשִּׁבֳּלִים** — *And I will glean among the ears of grain.*

Among the מַתְּנוֹת עֲנִיִּים, *gifts to the poor,* the Torah gives poor people the right to enter the fields at harvesttime and collect stray ears of grain not more than one or two together, that are left behind or dropped by the field hands.

☐ **אַחַר אֲשֶׁר אֶמְצָא־חֵן בְּעֵינָיו** — *After I find favor in someone's eyes.*

Wisely and cautiously, Ruth said that she would look for a farmer who looked at her kindly, and only then would she try to collect grain in his field. Although it is the right of poor people to do so, as explained above, she surmised correctly that not all farmers and fieldworkers treat the poor with the proper consideration.

3. וַתֵּלֶךְ וַתָּבוֹא וַתְּלַקֵּט — *So she went and came and gleaned.*

Did she go and glean, go back home, and then come back to glean again? Rather she first went to the field and did not glean. Instead she left markers and noted landmarks along the way so that she would be able to return home safely after a day of gleaning in the fields. After she felt secure that she would not get lost in a land that was new to her, she

הַקֹּצְרִים וַיִּקֶר מִקְרֶהָ חֶלְקַת הַשָּׂדֶה לְבֹעַז
ד אֲשֶׁר מִמִּשְׁפַּחַת אֱלִימֶלֶךְ: וְהִנֵּה־בֹעַז בָּא
מִבֵּית לֶחֶם וַיֹּאמֶר לַקּוֹצְרִים יְהוָה עִמָּכֶם
ה וַיֹּאמְרוּ לוֹ יְבָרֶכְךָ יְהוָה: וַיֹּאמֶר בֹּעַז
לְנַעֲרוֹ הַנִּצָּב עַל־הַקּוֹצְרִים לְמִי הַנַּעֲרָה
ו הַזֹּאת: וַיַּעַן הַנַּעַר הַנִּצָּב עַל־הַקּוֹצְרִים
וַיֹּאמַר נַעֲרָה מוֹאֲבִיָּה הִיא הַשָּׁבָה עִם־
ז נָעֳמִי מִשְּׂדֵי מוֹאָב: וַתֹּאמֶר אֲלַקֳטָה־נָּא

רש"י

ויקר מקרה. לבא בחלקת השדה אשר לבועז: **(ה) למי הנערה הזאת.** וכי דרכו של בועז לשאול בנשים, אלא דברי צניעות וחכמה ראה בה, שתי שבלים לקטה, שלשה אינה לקטה, והיתה מלקטת עומדות מעומד ושוכבות מיושב, כדי שלא תשחה: **(ו) השבה עם נעמי.** הטעם למעלה תחת השי"ן לפי שהוא לשון עבר ואינה לשון פועלת: **(ז) ותאמר.** בלבה: **אלקטה נא.** לקט השבלים:

went to the fields to glean food (*Rashi*). In addition, she wanted to be sure that she would not be lost and be secluded in a field with a man,which is inappropriate.

☐ **וַיִּקֶר מִקְרֶהָ** — *And He* [i.e., God] *made her happen upon . . .*

It was not her own doing that she "happened" upon the field that would change her destiny. Rather it was God Who guided her to the field and the person who would make her the "Mother of Royalty." Alternatively, the word מִקְרֶהָ is in the plural, implying that she tried several fields before she "happened upon" the one of her relative Boaz.

4. ה׳ עִמָּכֶם — *"HASHEM be with you."*

From the fact that Boaz addressed his workers with the Four-letter Name, the Sages (*Berachos* 54a) deduce that people should use His Name in greeting to show that it is important to greet one another in a friendly manner.

5. לְנַעֲרוֹ הַנִּצָּב עַל־הַקּוֹצְרִים — *To his worker who was overseeing the harvesters.*

While the foreman supervised the workers at the harvest, he also

the harvesters, and He made her happen upon a
parcel of land belonging to Boaz, who was of the
family of Elimelech.
4 *Behold, Boaz arrived from Bethlehem. He said*
to the harvesters, "Hashem be with you!" And
they answered him, "May Hashem bless you!"
5 *Boaz then said to his worker who was overseeing*
the harvesters, "To whom does that young
woman belong?" 6 *The worker who was over-*
seeing the harvesters replied, "She is a Moabite
girl, the one who returned with Naomi from the
fields of Moab; 7 *and she had said, 'Please let me*

---

made sure that the people gleaning ears of grain were truly poor. To let others glean would not only be stealing on their part, but it would deprive poor people of the food that was rightly theirs.

☐ לְמִי — *To whom . . . ?*

The Sages wonder: Was it the custom of Boaz to inquire about women? It is improper to do so (*Shabbos* 113b; *Rashi*). They explain that Boaz was impressed by Ruth's unusually honest and modest behavior. She gleaned only one or two stalks at a time, but never three, since poor people are entitled to not more than two together. Also, if a stalk had fallen to the ground, she did not bend to pick it up, because that would be immodest; instead she squatted. Seeing that she was an exceptional person, Boaz asked who she was.

7. וַתֹּאמֶר — *And she had said.*

To us. In other words, she informed the field laborers that she wished to glean in their field. Even though she did not need their permission, since the Torah gives all poor people the right to glean, she wanted to ascertain whether they would object. This was a further display of her refined manners.

According to *Rashi*, she did not verbalize this to anyone. The foreman thus told Boaz that Ruth had obviously decided to follow his men to glean in the field.

וְאָסַפְתִּ֣י בָֽעֳמָרִ֔ים אַחֲרֵ֖י הַקּֽוֹצְרִ֑ים וַתָּב֣וֹא
וַֽתַּעֲמ֗וֹד מֵאָ֤ז הַבֹּ֙קֶר֙ וְעַד־עַ֔תָּה זֶ֛ה שִׁבְתָּ֥הּ
ח הַבַּ֖יִת מְעָֽט׃ וַיֹּ֩אמֶר֩ בֹּ֨עַז אֶל־ר֜וּת הֲל֧וֹא
שָׁמַ֣עַתְּ בִּתִּ֗י אַל־תֵּֽלְכִי֙ לִלְקֹ֙ט֙ בְּשָׂדֶ֣ה אַחֵ֔ר
וְגַ֛ם לֹ֥א תַעֲבוּרִ֖י מִזֶּ֑ה וְכֹ֥ה תִדְבָּקִ֖ין עִם־
ט נַעֲרֹתָֽי׃ עֵינַ֜יִךְ בַּשָּׂדֶ֤ה אֲשֶׁר־יִקְצֹרוּן֙
וְהָלַ֣כְתְּ אַחֲרֵיהֶ֔ן הֲל֥וֹא צִוִּ֛יתִי אֶת־
הַנְּעָרִ֖ים לְבִלְתִּ֣י נָגְעֵ֑ךְ וְצָמִ֗ת וְהָלַכְתְּ֙ אֶל־

רש"י

ואספתי בעמרים. שכחה של עמרים: **(ט) וצמית והלכת אל הכלים.** ואם תצמאי אל תכלמי מללכת ולשתות מכלי המים אשר ישאבון הנערים:

☐ **וְאָסַפְתִּי בָעֳמָרִים** — *And gather among the sheaves.*

Here she was referring to שִׁכְחָה, a poor person's right to take sheaves that had been *forgotten* by the harvesters.

☐ **אַחֲרֵי הַקּוֹצְרִים** — *Behind the harvesters,*

But not in front of them, since the poor may not take anything until after the farmers and their laborers have gone through the rows of produce.

☐ **וַתַּעֲמוֹד** — *And she has stood.*

By saying that she had been in the field all day, the foreman meant to prove that none of his men had interfered with her or any of the other poor people who were gleaning in the field.

☐ **זֶה שִׁבְתָּהּ הַבַּיִת מְעָט** — *[Except] for her resting a little in the hut.*

This expression implies that she was in the hut as they spoke. Apparently Boaz had a hut in the field, for himself and his workers to rest and to find shelter from the hot sun. The men allowed Ruth to rest there, as well.

8. הֲלוֹא שָׁמַעַתְּ בִּתִּי — *Hear me well, my daughter.*

Boaz was surprised that she had gone to the hut, something that gleaners normally did not do. He encouraged her to feel that she was welcome in his field, and when his workers saw that he was so solicitous of her welfare, they would treat her very well.

2/ 8-9 *glean and gather among the sheaves behind the
harvesters.' So she came, and has stood since the
morning until now; [except for] her resting a little in
the hut."*
8 *Then Boaz said to Ruth, "Hear me well, my daughter. Do not go to glean in another field, and don't leave
here, but stay close to my maidens.* 9 *Keep your eyes
on the field which they are harvesting and follow after
them. I have ordered the [male] workers not to harm
you. Should you become thirsty, go to the jugs and*

By addressing her as *my daughter*, Boaz showed that he was receiving her with respect.

□ אַל־תֵּלְכִי — *Do not go . . .*

Do not go to other fields, because there is still much that you can glean in my field. Lest she think that he wanted her to stop gleaning anywhere — either in his field or in someone else's — Boaz hastened to add, *don't leave here*. The message was clear, as Boaz would tell his workers, that he wanted Ruth to stay in his field and glean enough to feed her mother-in-law and herself generously.

□ וְכֹה תִדְבָּקִין עִם־נַעֲרֹתָי — *But stay close to my maidens.*

Impressed though Boaz had been with Ruth's modesty, he still wondered whether she, as a woman from Moab, was sufficiently familiar with the customs of Israel, especially in the area of modesty. Since Boaz had women working in his fields, he urged Ruth to stay with them, rather than with the men.

9. אֲשֶׁר־יִקְצֹרוּן — *Which they are harvesting.*

In the previous verse, Boaz spoke of the maidens; here he speaks of the male workers. Both men and women worked in the field, each group having its own assignemnts. Ruth was to stay with the women, as Boaz said, that she should follow אַחֲרֵיהֶן, *after them*, in the feminine form.

□ לְבִלְתִּי נָגְעֵךְ — *Not to harm you..*

Targum renders this phrase as דְּלָא יִקְרְבוּן בִּיךְ, *not to approach you*. Thus, Boaz assured Ruth that not only would she not actually be harmed, she would not even have to deal with unwanted social interaction.

הַכֵּלִ֔ים וְשָׁתִ֕ית מֵאֲשֶׁ֥ר יִשְׁאֲב֖וּן הַנְּעָרִֽים׃
י וַתִּפֹּל֙ עַל־פָּנֶ֔יהָ וַתִּשְׁתַּ֖חוּ אָ֑רְצָה וַתֹּ֣אמֶר
אֵלָ֗יו מַדּ֩וּעַ֩ מָצָ֨אתִי חֵ֤ן בְּעֵינֶ֙יךָ֙ לְהַכִּירֵ֔נִי
יא וְאָנֹכִ֖י נָכְרִיָּֽה׃ וַיַּ֤עַן בֹּ֙עַז֙ וַיֹּ֣אמֶר לָ֔הּ הֻגֵּ֨ד
הֻגַּ֜ד לִ֗י כֹּ֤ל אֲשֶׁר־עָשִׂית֙ אֶת־חֲמוֹתֵ֔ךְ
אַחֲרֵ֖י מ֣וֹת אִישֵׁ֑ךְ וַתַּעַזְבִ֞י אָבִ֣יךְ וְאִמֵּ֗ךְ
וְאֶ֙רֶץ֙ מֽוֹלַדְתֵּ֔ךְ וַתֵּ֣לְכִ֔י אֶל־עַ֕ם אֲשֶׁ֥ר לֹא־
יב יָדַ֖עַתְּ תְּמ֥וֹל שִׁלְשֽׁוֹם׃ יְשַׁלֵּ֥ם יהוה פָּעֳלֵ֑ךְ

☐ **מֵאֲשֶׁר יִשְׁאֲבוּן הַנְּעָרִים** — *From what the young men have drawn.*

Even though the men drew water for their own needs, Boaz instructed them to share it with Ruth and draw more water for themselves if need be.

10. לְהַכִּירֵנִי — *That you should take special note of me.*

Ruth was overcome with gratitude at Boaz's gesture of concern for her plight, especially since she was a foreigner whose right to marry a Jew was in dispute. From the special consideration Boaz was showing her, Ruth inferred that Boaz considered her to be eligible to marry into the Jewish community. This surprised her because, as she went on to say.

☐ **וְאָנֹכִי נָכְרִיָּה** — *Though I am a foreigner.*

Ruth was surprised at Boaz, becaue she was a *foreigner*, i.e., even though she was a convert, she came from a nation whose people were not permitted to marry Jews. She implied that if Boaz was so friendly because "*I have found favor in your eyes,*" he would be disqualified halachically from ruling favorably on her status, since his personal affection would prevent him from being objective.

11. הֻגֵּד הֻגַּד לִי — *I have been fully informed.*

The plain meaning of Boaz's response was that he wanted to help her because he was impressed with her generosity and kindness to Naomi. *Targum*, however, interprets this as an answer to Ruth's surprise at his friendly treatment of someone who was forbidden to marry into the nation. *Targum* renders that *I have been fully informed* of the halachah that only male Moabite converts are forbidden to marry Jews, but that Moabite women face no such restrictions. Accordingly, it should not be surprising that he was so kind to Ruth.

drink from what the young men have drawn."

10 *Then she fell on her face, bowing down to the ground, and said to him, "Why have I found favor in your eyes that you should take special note of me though I am a foreigner?"*

11 *Boaz replied and said to her, "I have been fully informed of all that you have done for your mother-in-law after the death of your husband — how you left your father and mother and the land of your birth and went to a people you had not*
known yesterday or earlier. 12 *May Hashem*
reward your action, and may your payment be

☐ **כֹּל אֲשֶׁר־עָשִׂית** — *All that you have done.*

Targum renders that Boaz had been informed prophetically that Ruth would become the ancestress of Jewish monarchy. By speaking of her kindness to Naomi, Boaz alluded to the underlying reason that Moabite women were permitted to marry into the Jewish nation. King David said עוֹלָם חֶסֶד יִבָּנֶה, *The world is built upon kindness* (*Tehillim* 89:3), and the same is true of the Davidic dynasty. Therefore, it was critical that the "mother of royalty" be a woman who had demonstrated kindness. Ruth was such a woman, and it may well be that it was for her sake that God did not prohibit Moabite women from entering the congregation of Israel. Kindness and a sense of responsibility for others was what motivated the daughters of Lot to live with their father in order to provide for the future of society.

☐ **אֲשֶׁר לֹא־יָדַעַתְּ תְּמוֹל שִׁלְשֹׁם** — *You had not known yesterday or earlier.*

Not only did Ruth come to *Eretz Yisrael* to join a nation that was new to her, she also did not know that the correct interpretation of the halachah would permit her to marry a Jew, so that she did not know if there would be a relative she could marry.

12. **יְשַׁלֵּם ה׳ פָּעֳלֵךְ** — *May HASHEM reward your action.*

The *action* of a convert that is deserving of reward is his acknowledgment of Hashem's greatness and his desire to praise Him. Thus, the very fact that Ruth was ready to give up her entire past and come to

וּתְהִי מַשְׂכֻּרְתֵּךְ שְׁלֵמָה מֵעִם יהוה אֱלֹהֵי
יִשְׂרָאֵל אֲשֶׁר־בָּאת לַחֲסוֹת תַּחַת־כְּנָפָיו׃
יג וַתֹּאמֶר אֶמְצָא־חֵן בְּעֵינֶיךָ אֲדֹנִי כִּי
נִחַמְתָּנִי וְכִי דִבַּרְתָּ עַל־לֵב שִׁפְחָתֶךָ
יד וְאָנֹכִי לֹא אֶהְיֶה כְּאַחַת שִׁפְחֹתֶיךָ׃ וַיֹּאמֶר
לָה בֹעַז לְעֵת הָאֹכֶל גֹּשִׁי הֲלֹם וְאָכַלְתְּ מִן־

רש"י

(יג) לא אהיה כאחת שפחתך. אני חשובה כאחת מן השפחות שלך:

---

serve God was enough reason to entitle her to reward.

Her progeny carried on that legacy, as the Sages say of King David שֶׁרִוָּהוּ לְהקב״ה בְּשִׁירוֹת וְתִשְׁבָּחוֹת, *that He satiated the Holy One, Blessed is He, with songs and praises.* As noted above, this is alluded to in Ruth's name: the word Ruth [רות] is related to the word רִוָּהוּ, *satiated.*

☐ **שְׁלֵמָה** — *Full.*

This word alludes to שְׁלֹמֹה, *King Solomon.* The Midrash (*Yalkut Shimoni* 602) teaches that his name implies that the *fullness* of God's blessings upon Israel would be realized in the time of Solomon, as Scripture says of his reign, *not one word has gone unfulfilled from the entire gracious promise that He pronounced through His servant Moses* (*I Melachim* 8:56).

☐ **לַחֲסוֹת תַּחַת־כְּנָפָיו** — *Under Whose wings you have come to seek refuge.*

The implication of this term is passive: One who seeks refuge under God's wings is content to have faith in Him even if He does not actively perform miracles to protect the fugitive. So strong is such a person's faith that he would rather rely on God's refuge than trust human promises of support.

The word כָּנָף, *wing,* sometimes means *edge.* In this verse it can be seen to have both connotations. Ruth placed herself under the *wings* of the protection of God and His angels. At the same time she would sing God's praises, as Scripture states: מִכְּנַף הָאָרֶץ זְמִרֹת שָׁמַעְנוּ, *From the edge of the earth we have heard songs [of praise]* (*Yeshayahu* 24:16). This, too, was an allusion to David, whom God protected and who satiated

2/ 13-14 *full from Hashem, the God of Israel, under Whose*
wings you have come to seek refuge."
[13] *Then she said, "May I continue to find favor in*
your eyes, my lord, because you have comforted
me, and because you have spoken to the heart of
your maidservant, and I shall no longer be like
one of your maidservants." [14] *At mealtime, Boaz*
said to her, "Come over here and partake of the

God with praises.

13. אֶמְצָא־חֵן — *May I continue to find favor.*

Now that you have intimated that I am permitted to marry a Jew I hope that I will continue to find favor and actually be able to find a proper mate.

☐ **נִחַמְתָּנִי** — *You have comforted me,*

by telling me that I may become a full-fledged member of the nation.

☐ **וְכִי דִבַּרְתָּ עַל־לֵב שִׁפְחָתֶךָ** — *Because you have spoken to the heart of your maidservant.*

Generally, Scripture uses the word שִׁפְחָה to refer to a non-Jewish maidservant. Thus, Ruth was saying that she had thought that, regarding marriage, she was no better than a gentile maidservant, but Boaz had comforted her by saying that that was not the case, and therefore Ruth rejoiced and said . . .

☐ **וְאָנֹכִי לֹא אֶהְיֶה** — *I shall no longer be*

like one of the maidservants. Instead I can take my place among Jewish women as their equal.

14. לְעֵת הָאֹכֶל — *At mealtime.*

Boaz alluded to another, far more significant meal — her future, festive wedding feast.

☐ **גֹּשִׁי הֲלֹם** — *Come over here.*

The Sages (*Shabbos* 113b) teach that here again, Boaz alluded to Ruth's future descendant, King David. In his great modesty, David referred to his ascension to the throne as מִי אָנֹכִי . . . כִּי הֲבִיאֹתַנִי עַד־הֲלֹם, *Who am I . . . that You should have brought me over here [i.e., this far]* (*II Shmuel* 7:18).

הַלֶּ֗חֶם וְטָבַ֥לְתְּ פִּתֵּ֖ךְ בַּחֹ֑מֶץ וַתֵּ֙שֶׁב֙ מִצַּ֣ד
הַקֹּֽצְרִ֔ים וַיִּצְבָּט־לָ֣הּ קָלִ֔י וַתֹּ֥אכַל וַתִּשְׂבַּ֖ע
טו וַתֹּתַֽר׃ וַתָּ֖קָם לְלַקֵּ֑ט וַיְצַו֩ בֹּ֨עַז אֶת־נְעָרָ֜יו
לֵאמֹ֗ר גַּ֣ם בֵּ֧ין הָֽעֳמָרִ֛ים תְּלַקֵּ֖ט וְלֹ֥א
טז תַכְלִימֽוּהָ׃ וְגַ֛ם שֹׁל־תָּשֹׁ֥לּוּ לָ֖הּ מִן־

רש"י

(יד) וטבלת פתך בחומץ. מכאן שהחומץ יפה לשרב: **ויצבט לה קלי.** ויושט לה, ואין לו דמיון במקרא אלא בלשון משנה (חגיגה כ, ב) אחוריים ותוך ובית הצביטה: **(טז) וגם של תשלו.** שכוח תשכחו, עשו עצמיכם כאילו אתם שוכחים, תרגום של שגגה שלותא, וכן (שמואל-ב ו,ז) על השל. ד"א לשון (דברים כח, מ) כי ישל זיתך:

☐ **מִן־הַלֶּחֶם** — *Of the bread,*

i.e., of the meal. *Bread* is usually used as a metaphor for the entire meal.

☐ **וְטָבַלְתְּ פִּתֵּךְ בַּחֹמֶץ** — *And dip your morsel in the vinegar.*

Vinegar is bitter, and, as the Sages comment, leaders should always feel as if they are bearing a box of vermin, lest they become arrogant. Commenting on the plain sense of the verse, the Sages (*Shabbos* 113b) comment יָפֶה חֹמֶץ לַשָּׁרָב, *vinegar is good in hot weather.* Allegorically, this means that the heated passion of the evil inclination can be mitigated by a realization that no one has a right to be arrogant, not even the most distinguished leaders.

The word בַּחֹמֶץ can be read בְּחָמֵץ, *with chametz*, which means leaven, but is also used in rabbinic literature to symbolize something that has a bad effect or that is undesirable. In the context of the above dictum of the Sages, the implication is that although a king always has a temptation to be arrogant, Hashem built in a protection against this in the case of the Davidic dynasty. The danger would be mitigated by the "*leaven*" in David's background, beginning with the union of Judah and Tamar, and He furthered it through the marriage of Boaz and Ruth, David's great-grandparents. It was a marriage that many people criticized — even claiming it to be a violation of Halachah — because of Ruth's Moabite lineage.

☐ **וַיִּצְבָּט־לָהּ קָלִי** —*He handed her parched grain.*

bread, and dip your morsel in the vinegar." So she sat beside the harvesters. He handed her parched grain, and she ate and was satisfied, and had some left over.

[15] Then she got up to glean, and Boaz ordered
his young men, saying, "Let her glean even
among the sheaves; do not embarrass her. [16] And
even deliberately pull out some for her from the

It may be that the word וַיִּצְבָּט refers to something that is handed to someone who is at a distance. The laborers were between Boaz and Ruth, and he handed the grain to her without approaching her closely. Apparently he gave this to her before the meal began and this was all she ate. It was all she needed, as the verse continues . . .

☐ וַתֹּאכַל וַתִּשְׂבַּע וַתֹּתַר— *She ate and was satisfied, and had some left over.*

This alludes to her righteous royal descendants, who were satisfied with small portions of food. For example, King Chizkiyahu's meal was a small portion of vegetables. He did not indulge himself with sumptuous banquets so that he could use his time to serve God.

15. גַּם בֵּין הָעֳמָרִים תְּלַקֵּט — *"Let her glean even among the sheaves."*

This implies that she would be gleaning even more sheaves than the Torah grants to the poor. This seems difficult since, as noted above, Boaz observed her and saw that she would pick up two sheaves, which the halachah permits, but she would not touch three fallen sheaves. Since she was careful to take only what was permitted, why was it necessary to instruct the young men regarding something that she would not do in any case? Perhaps the word עֳמָרִים, *sheaves*, refers to large bundles, which gleaners are not allowed to take. While Boaz saw that she tried to be careful not to glean what was not permitted, he thought that she may not have known all the laws, so he instructed his men that even if she picked up what she was not entitled to, they should not rebuke her.

16. וְגַם שֹׁל־תָּשֹׁלּוּ לָהּ — *And even deliberately pull out some for her.*

God rewards a farmer for the stalks of grain gleaned by the poor, even

הַצְּבָתִים וַעֲזַבְתֶּם וְלִקְּטָה וְלֹא תִגְעֲרוּ־בָהּ׃
יז וַתְּלַקֵּט בַּשָּׂדֶה עַד־הָעָרֶב וַתַּחְבֹּט אֵת
יח אֲשֶׁר־לִקֵּטָה וַיְהִי כְּאֵיפָה שְׂעֹרִים׃ וַתִּשָּׂא
וַתָּבוֹא הָעִיר וַתֵּרֶא חֲמוֹתָהּ אֵת אֲשֶׁר־
לִקֵּטָה וַתּוֹצֵא וַתִּתֶּן־לָהּ אֵת אֲשֶׁר־הוֹתִרָה
יט מִשָּׂבְעָהּ׃ וַתֹּאמֶר לָהּ חֲמוֹתָהּ אֵיפֹה לִקַּטְתְּ
הַיּוֹם וְאָנָה עָשִׂית יְהִי מַכִּירֵךְ בָּרוּךְ וַתַּגֵּד
לַחֲמוֹתָהּ אֵת אֲשֶׁר־עָשְׂתָה עִמּוֹ וַתֹּאמֶר
שֵׁם הָאִישׁ אֲשֶׁר עָשִׂיתִי עִמּוֹ הַיּוֹם בֹּעַז׃

רש"י

צבתים. עמרים קטנים. ויש דוגמתו בלשון משנה (עירובין נה, א) מלאן צבתים או כריכות: **(יט) יהי מכירך ברוך.** בעל השדה שנשא ונתן לך פנים ללקט בשדהו:

though the farmer does not leave anything for them and may not know that anything has fallen. Boaz went further. He wanted his workers to leave stalks intentionally. For this he would surely be rewarded, because he was enabling the poor to glean food without being embarrassed by the knowledge that he was leaving it for them.

☐ **הַצְּבָתִים** — *The bundles,*

i.e., the small bundles which the poor may take if they are forgotten in the field [שִׁכְחָה].

☐ **וְלֹא תִגְעֲרוּ־בָהּ** — *Don't rebuke her.*

This order would seem to be unnecessary, since Boaz had just told his men to permit her to glean and even to leave food for her intentionally. Why, then, would they think of rebuking her? Apparently he was merely reiterating what he said in the previous verse, to impress upon them that he wanted Ruth to be treated with the utmost sympathetic consideration.

17. וַיְהִי כְּאֵיפָה שְׂעֹרִים — *It was about an ephah of barley.*

This was three *se'ah* of grain, which was enough to feed Naomi and Ruth for five days, an unusual amount of grain for one day's gleaning.

bundles and leave them for her to glean; don't
rebuke her."
17 *So she gleaned in the field until evening, and*
she beat out what she had gleaned; it was about an
ephah of barley. 18 *She carried it and came to the*
city. Her mother-in-law saw what she had gleaned,
and she took out and gave her what she had left
over after eating her fill.
19 *"Where did you glean today?" her mother-in-*
law asked her. "And where did you work? May the
one that took [such generous] notice of you be
blessed." So she told her mother-in-law by whom
she had worked, and said, "The name of the man
by whom I worked today is Boaz."

---

18. וַתֵּרֶא חֲמוֹתָהּ אֵת אֲשֶׁר־לִקֵּטָה — *Her mother-in-law saw what she had gleaned.*

Naomi was surprised at the large amount. Either a farmer had allowed Ruth to take so much or she had mistakenly gleaned more than was permitted. Therefore, without showing disapproval, in the next verse Naomi inquired what had happened.

19. אֵיפֹה לִקַּטְתְּ הַיּוֹם — *Where did you glean today,*

i.e., where did you glean לֶקֶט, *permissible gleanings*?

☐ **וְאָנָה עָשִׂית** — *And where did you work?*

Since you gathered so much food, a farmer must have made a gift to you in return for a favor. What *work* did you do for him and who is he?

☐ **אֲשֶׁר עָשִׂיתִי עִמּוֹ** — *By whom I worked.*

Ruth said nothing about the day's gleaning; she spoke only about the farm where she *worked*. Apparently she knew full well that Boaz had arranged for her to get such a large amount of barley. The Sages teach that the poor person does more for his benefactor than his benefactor does for him, because he provides the wealthy man with the opportunity to earn the great reward for giving charity. Therefore, poor people from worthy families used to say that they provided a source of merit for generous people.

כ וַתֹּאמֶר נָעֳמִי לְכַלָּתָהּ בָּרוּךְ הוּא לַיהוָה
אֲשֶׁר לֹא־עָזַב חַסְדּוֹ אֶת־הַחַיִּים וְאֶת־
הַמֵּתִים וַתֹּאמֶר לָהּ נָעֳמִי קָרוֹב לָנוּ
כא הָאִישׁ מִגֹּאֲלֵנוּ הוּא׃ וַתֹּאמֶר רוּת
הַמּוֹאֲבִיָּה גַּם ׀ כִּי־אָמַר אֵלַי עִם־הַנְּעָרִים
אֲשֶׁר־לִי תִּדְבָּקִין עַד אִם־כִּלּוּ אֵת כָּל־
כב הַקָּצִיר אֲשֶׁר־לִי׃ וַתֹּאמֶר נָעֳמִי אֶל־רוּת
כַּלָּתָהּ טוֹב בִּתִּי כִּי תֵצְאִי עִם־נַעֲרוֹתָיו וְלֹא
כג יִפְגְּעוּ־בָךְ בְּשָׂדֶה אַחֵר׃ וַתִּדְבַּק בְּנַעֲרוֹת
בֹּעַז לְלַקֵּט עַד־כְּלוֹת קְצִיר־הַשְּׂעֹרִים
וּקְצִיר הַחִטִּים וַתֵּשֶׁב אֶת־חֲמוֹתָהּ׃

רש"י

(כ) את החיים ואת המתים. שזן ומפרנס את החיים וטפל בצורכי המתים:

20. **בָּרוּךְ הוּא לַה׳** — *Blessed is he to* H*ASHEM.*

She did not say that Boaz is blessed *by* Hashem. Her expression implies that it is a blessing to Hashem that He has a servant like Boaz, a man who follows in God's ways of kindness and generosity.

☐ **אֶת־הַחַיִּים וְאֶת־הַמֵּתִים** — *With the living and with the dead.*

Naomi and Ruth were the *living*, who were now benefiting from God's kindness, through His servant Boaz. The *dead* were Elimelech and his sons, for whom Naomi had been able to obtain proper burial shrouds. This verse teaches us a profound lesson: When a person has a kindness done to him, in addition to a person's thanking his benefactor, he must also thank God. Here, Boaz did kindness to Ruth and Naomi, and Naomi is expressing her thanks to God.

In addition, while she is thanking Him for the kindness that was done to her now, she is reiterating her thanks to Him for having provided for her years earlier, when she was able to bring her husband and sons to proper burial.

☐ **מִגֹּאֲלֵנוּ הוּא** — *He is one of our redeeming kinsmen.*

A "redeemer" is a relative who has the moral responsibility to *redeem*,

20 *Naomi said to her daughter-in-law, "Blessed is he
to Hashem, Who has not failed in His kindness with
the living and with the dead!" Naomi then said to
her, "The man is closely related to us; he is one of
our redeeming kinsmen."*
21 *And Ruth the Moabite said, "What's more, he
even said to me, 'Stay close to my workers, until
they have finished all my harvest.' "* 22 *Naomi said
to her daughter-in-law Ruth, "It is fine, my
daughter, that you go out with his maidens, so
that you will not be annoyed in another field."*
23 *So she stayed close to Boaz's maidens to glean,
until the end of the barley harvest and of the wheat
harvest. Then she stayed [at home] with her
mother-in-law.*

---

i.e., buy back, a property that a family member was forced to sell due to his poverty (see *Vayikra* 25:23-34). Although Boaz was not the closest relative (see below), he would be next in line if the closest relative could not or would not buy back Elimelech's property and give the money to Naomi in payment for her *kesubah* and Ruth's. Although Ruth was not owed a *kesubah* since her marriage to Machlon was not halachically valid, nevertheless Machlon had surely promised her a settlement.

21. עִם־הַנְּעָרִים — *My workers.*

Ruth did not quote Boaz correctly: this word is the masculine, but Boaz told her to *stay close to my maidens* (v. 8). Ruth surely did not lack modesty; she merely did not express herself exactly.

22. עִם־נַעֲרוֹתָיו — *With his maidens.*

Realizing that Boaz must have told Ruth to stay with the girls, Naomi gently corrected her.

23. וַתֵּשֶׁב אֶת־חֲמוֹתָהּ — *Then she stayed [at home] with her mother-in-law.*

Ruth heeded the advice of Boaz and Naomi. She stayed with the maidens. She remained single, and Naomi was thus still her mother-in-law.

א וַתֹּאמֶר לָהּ נָעֳמִי חֲמוֹתָהּ בִּתִּי הֲלֹא
ב אֲבַקֶּשׁ־לָךְ מָנוֹחַ אֲשֶׁר יִיטַב־לָךְ: ב וְעַתָּה
הֲלֹא בֹעַז מֹדַעְתָּנוּ אֲשֶׁר הָיִית אֶת־
נַעֲרוֹתָיו הִנֵּה־הוּא זֹרֶה אֶת־גֹּרֶן הַשְּׂעֹרִים
ג הַלָּיְלָה: ג וְרָחַצְתְּ ׀ וָסַכְתְּ וְשַׂמְתְּ °שמלתך

°שִׂמְלֹתַיִךְ ק

רש"י

(ב) מדעתנו. קרובנו: **הנה הוא זורה.** המוץ, ווכטו"ר בלע"ז: **הלילה.** שהיה הדור פרוץ בגנבה וגזל והיה ישן בגורנו לשמור גורנו: **(ג) ורחצת.** מטנוף ע"ז שלך: **וסכת.** אלו מצות: **ושמת שמלותיך.** בגדים של שבת:

Chapter 3

1. **נָעֳמִי חֲמוֹתָהּ** — *Naomi, her mother-in-law.*

Naomi has a plan to persuade Boaz to marry Ruth in a form of levirate marriage [*yibum*]. Were this to happen, the name of Machlon, Ruth's first husband, would remain alive, as it were, and Naomi could continue to consider Ruth her daughter-in-law.

□ **מָנוֹחַ** — *Security.*

Naomi reiterated the hope she expressed when both of her sons died and she decided to return to *Eretz Yisrael.* At that time, she urged both Ruth and Orpah to return to their mothers' homes, where they would find husbands and מְנוּחָה, *security* (1:9). Now that God had orchestrated events so that there was hope that Ruth could marry Boaz, Naomi once again showed her concern for her daughter-in-law's future.

Naomi may also have been alluding to Manoach, the future father of Samson, since the name Manoach, מָנוֹחַ, is related to the word מְנוּחָה, *security* or *rest.* The Sages *(Bava Basra* 91a) teach that Boaz made a hundred-twenty feasts to celebrate the marriages of his thirty sons and thirty daughters, but they all died in his lifetime because he snubbed Manoach and did not invite him to any of the celebrations. Boaz said, "He is childless and will not invite me to any marriages. Why should I invite him to my celebrations?" Knowing of these tragedies, Naomi alluded to the need to make peace with Manoach, so that the same tragedy would not befall Ruth, if, indeed, Boaz would marry her. In the end, they married and Manoach was invited, and their son Oved survived.

[1] *Naomi, her mother-in-law, said to her, "My*
daughter, I must seek security for you, that it may
go well with you. [2] *Now, Boaz, our relative, with*
whose maidens you have been, will be winnowing
barley tonight on the threshing floor. [3] *Therefore,*
bathe and anoint yourself, don your garments, and

---

2. מֹדַעְתָּנוּ — *Our relative,*

i.e., he is our redeemer.

☐ הִנֵּה־הוּא זֹרֶה . . . הַלָּיְלָה — *Will be winnowing . . . tonight.*

Although it was the winnowing season, which is why Boaz was spending so much time in the field, he surely was not winnowing in the dark of night. The reason he slept in the field, *Rashi* comments, is to protect his property from robbers, since the crop was fully grown and tempting to potential thieves.

3. שִׂמְלֹתַיִךְ — *Your garments,*

i.e., your finest Shabbos clothing. Obviously, Ruth had been dressed whenever she went to the fields to glean, but now Naomi wanted her to be as attractive as possible (*Rashi*).

Since whatever Ruth had been wearing up to then was surely hers, why did Naomi seem to be stressing that the garments should be *yours*? In the context of the rule that one should dress especially well for Shabbos, the Talmud (*Shabbos* 113a) quotes R' Yochanan who referred to his clothing as לְמָאנֵיה מְכַבְּדוּתַי, *the things that honor me.* The implication is that Shabbos clothing — unlike weekday work clothes — honor the one who wears them. Naomi, therefore, urged Ruth to wear the garments that would make *her* feel honored, and that is a matter of personal taste.

The word is spelled in the singular, שִׂמְלָתֵךְ, *your garment,* because there was a difference between what Naomi suggested to Ruth and what Ruth decided to do. On the Sabbath it is customary to wear many garments in honor of the day, and by speaking in the plural, Naomi suggested that Ruth should don all of her finery. When going to work — in this case, gleaning — someone would wear a single, practical garment, because ornamental garments would get in the way. Ruth put on only one garment for the walk to the field, and dressed in her Sabbath finery after she got there (see v. 6).

עָלַיִךְ °וירדתי הַגֹּרֶן אַל־תִּוָּדְעִי לָאִישׁ עַד
°וְיָרַדְתְּ ק׳ ד כַּלֹּתוֹ לֶאֱכֹל וְלִשְׁתּוֹת: וִיהִי בְשָׁכְבוֹ וְיָדַעַתְּ
אֶת־הַמָּקוֹם אֲשֶׁר יִשְׁכַּב־שָׁם וּבָאת וְגִלִּית
°וְשָׁכָבְתְּ ק׳ מַרְגְּלֹתָיו °ושכבתי וְהוּא יַגִּיד לָךְ אֵת אֲשֶׁר
ה תַּעֲשִׂין: וַתֹּאמֶר אֵלֶיהָ כֹּל אֲשֶׁר־תֹּאמְרִי
°אֵלַי ק׳ ו [°אלי] אֶעֱשֶׂה: וַתֵּרֶד הַגֹּרֶן וַתַּעַשׂ כְּכֹל
ז אֲשֶׁר־צִוַּתָּה חֲמוֹתָהּ: וַיֹּאכַל בֹּעַז וַיֵּשְׁתְּ

רש"י

וירדת הגורן. וירדתי כתיב, זכותי תרד עמך: **אל תודעי לאיש.** לבועז: (ו) **ותרד הגורן ותעש.** היא אמרה לה ורחצת וסכת ושמת שמלותיך עליך ואחר כך וירדת הגורן, והיא לא עשתה כן, אלא אמרה אם ארד כשאני מקושטת הפוגע בי והרואה אותי יאמר שאני זונה, לפיכך ירדה בתחלה הגורן ואחר כך קשטה את עצמה כאשר צותה חמותה: (ז) **וייטב לבו.** עסק בתורה:

☐ **וְיָרַדְתְּ** — *And go down.*

Although the word is read [קְרִי] in the second person, *[you] go down,* it is spelled וְיָרַדְתִּי, *I will go down*, as if Naomi was saying that she herself would go down to the threshing floor. As noted above, although Naomi was concerned for Ruth's future, she was also thinking of her own destiny, because if Ruth was successful, Naomi's own son Machlon would be remembered.

☐ **אַל־תִּוָּדְעִי לָאִישׁ** — *Do not make yourself known to the man.*

The prefix לָ, *to the*, indicates that Naomi had one specific man in mind. She could not have meant that not a single person should know that Ruth was walking to the threshing floor, since she would be walking on a public road and was bound to be observed by at least some people. Rather, Naomi wanted Ruth to be sure that Boaz would not see her until the rest of her plan was put into action.

4. **וְשָׁכָבְתְּ** — *And lie down.*

Here, too, the word is spelled in the first person, וְשָׁכַבְתִּי, *And I will lie down*, because Ruth would be acting vicariously on Naomi's behalf. By lying down near Boaz, Ruth would be symbolizing the hope that Boaz would marry her and they would have a child together. Obviously this would not apply to Naomi in the literal sense, but, as the end of the Book

go down to the threshing floor, but do not make
yourself known to the man until he has finished
eating and drinking. 4 *And when he lies down, note*
the place where he lies, and go over, uncover his feet,
and lie down. And he will tell you what you are to
do." 5 *She replied, "All that you say [to me] I will do."*
6 *So she went down to the threshing floor*
and did everything as her mother-in-law
instructed her. 7 *Boaz ate and drank and his*

---

shows, Ruth's child was regarded as if he was Naomi's as well. In the figurative sense, therefore, it was as if Naomi herself would be marrying Boaz, since a grandmother feels a grandchild is like her own. Naomi herself would not consider marrying her cousin Boaz because she was too old to have children, as she said in 1:11.

□ וְהוּא יַגִּיד לָךְ — *And he will tell you.*

Even though this would be a test of Boaz's rectitude, you can rely on him not to tell you to do anything improper.

5. כֹּל אֲשֶׁר־תֹּאמְרִי [אֵלַי] אֶעֱשֶׂה — *"All that you say [to me] I will do."*

The word אֵלַי, *to me,* is read, but it does not appear in the text. The written word is omitted to imply that even though Naomi had Ruth's benefit in mind, Ruth did not think of herself at all. She promised to carry out the instructions purely for the sake of Naomi.

6. וַתֵּרֶד הַגֹּרֶן וַתַּעַשׂ — *So she went down to the threshing floor and [only then] did . . .*

As noted (v. 3) Naomi's instructions were for Ruth to beautify herself and don her finery first, and only then go to the threshing floor. The order of this verse indicates that she did the reverse. Ruth reasoned that if she were to make all her preparations at home and walked down the roads dressed in her best, anyone who saw her would accuse her of having immoral intentions. Instead, she went to the threshing floor in her weekday clothing and only then dressed in her finery (*Rashi*).

We may assume that Naomi, too, meant that Ruth should don her best clothing only when she got to the threshing floor. She had no need to say so explicitly because she knew that Ruth was too righteous and wise to go through the streets calling attention to herself.

וַיִּיטַב לִבּוֹ וַיָּבֹא לִשְׁכַּב בִּקְצֵה הָעֲרֵמָה
ח וַתָּבֹא בַלָּט וַתְּגַל מַרְגְּלֹתָיו וַתִּשְׁכָּב׃ וַיְהִי
בַּחֲצִי הַלַּיְלָה וַיֶּחֱרַד הָאִישׁ וַיִּלָּפֵת וְהִנֵּה
ט אִשָּׁה שֹׁכֶבֶת מַרְגְּלֹתָיו׃ וַיֹּאמֶר מִי־אָתְּ
וַתֹּאמֶר אָנֹכִי רוּת אֲמָתֶךָ וּפָרַשְׂתָּ כְנָפֶךָ
י עַל־אֲמָתְךָ כִּי גֹאֵל אָתָּה׃ וַיֹּאמֶר בְּרוּכָה
אַתְּ לַיהוה בִּתִּי הֵיטַבְתְּ חַסְדֵּךְ הָאַחֲרוֹן

רש"י

ותבא בלט. בנחת: **(ח) ויחרד האיש.** כסבור שד הוא ובקש לזעוק והיא אחזתו ולפפתו בזרועותיה: **וילפת.** ויאחז כמו (שופטים טז, כט) וילפת שמשון: **והנה אשה.** נתן ידו על ראשה והכיר שהיא אשה: **(ט) ופרשת כנפך.** כנף בגדך לכסותי בטליתך, והוא לשון נישואין: **כי גואל אתה.** לגאול נחלת אישי, כמו שנאמר (ויקרא כה, כה) ובא גואלו הקרוב אליו וגאל וגו', והמותי ואני צריכות למכור נחלתנו, ועתה עליך לקנות, קנה גם אותי עמה שיזכר שם המת על נחלתו, כשאבא על השדה יאמרו זאת אשת מחלון: **(י) מן הראשון.** אשר עשית עם חמותך:

---

7. וַיִּיטַב לִבּוֹ — *And his heart was merry.*

It is not logical to say that a man of his stature would be made merry by food and drink, nor would that be a reason for Scripture to mention it. Therefore *Rashi* cites the Midrash that after having his evening meal Boaz had the pleasure of studying Torah. Scripture mentions this to teach that it is good to study Torah after a meal, since one will be able to concentrate better if one is not distracted by hunger.

8. וַיִּלָּפֵת — *And he was grasped.*

She had grasped him so that he would realize that she was not a man — since he slept there to protect his crop from thieves — and that she was not some sort of demon.

□ **וְהִנֵּה אִשָּׁה** — *And behold! it was a woman.*

Perhaps he could tell that the hand holding him was a woman's, or, as *Rashi* comments, he felt her head and realized that it was that of a woman.

9. וּפָרַשְׂתָּ כְנָפֶךָ — *Spread your robe.*

In the plain sense of the word, she intimated that he should spread his robe over her in the sense of a marriage canopy [*chupah*]. Alter-

heart was merry. He went to lie down at the
end of the grain pile, and she came stealthily,
uncovered his feet, and lay down. 8 *In the*
middle of the night the man was startled, and
he was grasped — and behold! it was a
woman lying at his feet!
9 *He said, "Who are you?" And she*
answered, "I am your handmaid, Ruth.
Spread your robe over your handmaid, for
you are a redeemer."
10 *And he said, "You are blessed of Hashem,*
my daughter; you have made your latest act of
kindness greater than the first, in that you

---

natively, she meant that he should spread his protective cloak over her, like a husband protecting his wife.

☐ כִּי גֹאֵל אָתָּה — *For you are a redeemer.*

Since you are a close relative, it is incumbent upon you to redeem the property of Machlon. And while you are redeeming the field, you should "redeem" me as well and marry me (*Rashi*). Alternatively, in the case of the Torah's commandment of *yibum* [levirate marriage], which applies to a brother of the deceased, the marriage is consummated when they simply live together, even without witnesses. Since Boaz was not a brother of Machlon, he would have to marry Ruth in the normal manner, with *kiddushin* and witnesses. Ruth's request was that he, as a relative, should take upon himself an obligation to redeem the field and marry her. She knew that nothing improper would happen that night since they would be able to marry the next day.

10. הֵיטַבְתְּ חַסְדֵּךְ הָאַחֲרוֹן— *You have made your latest act of kindness greater.*

Your request now that I, an old man, become your husband is a greater act of kindness than what you have done for your mother-in-law. You are still a young woman and anyone would expect you to seek to marry a much younger man — even if he is poor, and certainly if he is rich.

☐ מִן־הָרִאשׁוֹן — *than the first.*

Your first kindness was what you did for Naomi, but that was pri-

מִן־הָרִאשׁוֹן לְבִלְתִּי־לֶכֶת אַחֲרֵי הַבַּחוּרִים
יא אִם־דַּל וְאִם־עָשִׁיר׃ וְעַתָּה בִּתִּי אַל־תִּירְאִי
כֹּל אֲשֶׁר־תֹּאמְרִי אֶעֱשֶׂה־לָּךְ כִּי יוֹדֵעַ כָּל־
יב שַׁעַר עַמִּי כִּי אֵשֶׁת חַיִל אָתְּ׃ וְעַתָּה כִּי
אָמְנָם כִּי [אם כתיב ולא קרי] גֹאֵל אָנֹכִי וְגַם יֵשׁ
יג גֹּאֵל קָרוֹב מִמֶּנִּי׃ לִינִי ׀ הַלַּיְלָה וְהָיָה
בַבֹּקֶר אִם־יִגְאָלֵךְ טוֹב יִגְאָל וְאִם־לֹא

רש"י

(יב) ועתה כי אמנם. אם כתיב ולא קרי, כלומר משמע ספק, ודאי **יש גואל קרוב ממני.** (ס"א אם משמע ספק והוא ודאי.) אמר רבי יהושע בן לוי, שלמון ואלימלך וטוב אחים היו ומהו אשר לאחינו לאלימלך לעולם קורא אדם את דודו אחיו כענין שנאמר (בראשית יד, יד) וישמע אברם כי נשבה אחיו, והלא אברהם דודו היה, כך היה בועז לאלימלך בן אחיו, קרובו של מחלון, אבל טוב היה קרוב יותר: **קרוב ממני.** שהוא אח ואני בן אח: **(יג) ליני הלילה.** ליני בלא איש: **חי ה'.** אמרה לו בדברים אתה מוליאני, קפץ ונשבע לה שאינה מוליאה בדברים. ויש מרבותינו אמרו (ספרי בהעלותך פח) ליצרו נשבע, שהיה יצרו מקטרגו אתה פנוי והיא פנויה, בוא עליה, ונשבע שלא יבא עליה אלא על ידי נישואין:

marily a monetary favor, in that you accepted a life of poverty for her sake. But that sacrifice was financial. Now you are giving up the opportunity for a normal marriage, and that is a greater sacrifice.

11. אַל־תִּירְאִי — *Do not fear.*

Do not be afraid that I will find some excuse to dismiss your request.

☐ **כֹּל אֲשֶׁר־תֹּאמְרִי** — *Whatever you say.*

Boaz would soon tell her that there was a relative who was closer than he, and who therefore had the primary responsibility to be the redeemer. He was now assuring her that if she refused to accept that redeemer, he, Boaz, would comply with her wish and find a way to become the redeemer.

☐ **אֶעֱשֶׂה־לָּךְ**— *I will do for you.*

When the matter of the primary redeemer is settled, I will marry you, or, if you would rather marry a younger man, I will help you find one.

☐ **כִּי אֵשֶׁת חַיִל אָתְּ** — *That you are a worthy woman.*

After first assuring her that he would help her whatever course she

have not gone after the younger men, be they poor
or rich. 11 *And now, my daughter, do not fear;*
whatever you say, I will do for you; for all the men
in the gate of my people know that you are a
worthy woman. 12 *Now while it is true that I am a*
redeemer, there is also another redeemer closer than
I. 13 *Stay the night, then it will be in the morning, if*
Tov will redeem you, let him redeem. But if he does

---

chose, Boaz said that she had proven herself as a *worthy woman* who would accept the will of God whatever it was. Therefore, since she had said that she was ready to marry the elderly Boaz, he was confident that she would agree to become the wife of the closer relative, if he was willing to marry her.

12. כִּי גֹאֵל אָנֹכִי — *That I am a redeemer.*

The text of the Book includes the word אִם — כִּי אִם — which is written, but not read. The extra word gives the phrase a sense of finality. Although, as Boaz told Ruth, he was second on the list of potential redeemers, he was certain that the closer relative would forgo the privilege and leave it to Boaz to be *the* redeemer who would actually purchase the property and marry her. Consequently, it was easy for Boaz to restrain any desire he might have, since he could "tell" himself that he would marry her very soon. However, when he spoke to Ruth, Boaz omitted the word אִם because of the possibility that the most eligible redeemer might surprise him and wish to marry Ruth.

13. לִינִי הַלַּיְלָה — *Stay the night.*

He meant to say that she should stay in the field that night, but without the company of a man, i.e., husband (*Rashi*).

☐ **וְהָיָה** — *Then it will be.*

This word has the same letters as Hashem's Four-letter Name. By using this word, Boaz was intimating that in the morning it would be God's will that the law will become known that a Moabite woman is permitted to marry a Jew.

☐ **אִם־יִגְאָלֵךְ טוֹב יִגְאָל** — *If Tov will redeem you, let him redeem.*

The redeemer, whose name was Tov, was an uncle of Naomi, and therefore had priority over Boaz, who was a cousin.

יַחְפֹּץ לְגָאֳלֵךְ וּגְאַלְתִּיךְ אָנֹכִי חַי־יְהוָה
יד שִׁכְבִי עַד־הַבֹּקֶר׃ וַתִּשְׁכַּב °מרגלותו עַד־ °מַרְגְּלוֹתָיו ק
הַבֹּקֶר וַתָּקָם °בטרום יַכִּיר אִישׁ אֶת־ °בְּטֶרֶם ק
רֵעֵהוּ וַיֹּאמֶר אַל־יִוָּדַע כִּי־בָאָה הָאִשָּׁה
טו הַגֹּרֶן׃ וַיֹּאמֶר הָבִי הַמִּטְפַּחַת אֲשֶׁר־עָלַיִךְ
וְאֶחֳזִי־בָהּ וַתֹּאחֶז בָּהּ וַיָּמָד שֵׁשׁ־שְׂעֹרִים
טז וַיָּשֶׁת עָלֶיהָ וַיָּבֹא הָעִיר׃ וַתָּבוֹא אֶל־
חֲמוֹתָהּ וַתֹּאמֶר מִי־אַתְּ בִּתִּי וַתַּגֶּד־לָהּ

רש"י

(יד) **ויאמר אל יודע.** מוסב על ותקם בטרם יכיר, הוא זרז לקום כי אמר בלבו אין כבודי שיודע **כי באה האשה הגורן:** (טו) **שש שעורים.** אי אפשר לומר שש סאין, שאין דרכה של אשה לשאת כמשאוי זה, אלא שש שעורים ממש, ורמז לה שעתיד לצאת ממנה בן שמתברך בשש ברכות, רוח חכמה ובינה, עצה וגבורה, רוח דעת ויראת ה':

☐ **שִׁכְבִי עַד־הַבֹּקֶר** — *Lie down until the morning.*

Although, as noted above, the word שִׁכְבִי implies a marital relationship, Boaz was not suggesting that they should live together that night. Rather, he may have used this term to reassure her that she could be certain that she would be married very soon, either to him or to Tov, so that she could feel as secure as if she was married.

14. וַתִּשְׁכַּב מַרְגְּלוֹתָיו — *So she lay at his feet.*

Since she was now confident that her status would be settled in the morning, she was content to lie at his feet.

☐ **בְּטֶרֶם יַכִּיר אִישׁ אֶת־רֵעֵהוּ** — *Before one man could recognize another.*

Thus she would leave shortly after the first glimmering of light [עֲלוֹת הַשַּׁחַר], when there would be a bit of light to help her find her way back home, but before anyone could recognize her and raise questions about where she had spent the night. None of the fieldworkers were there as yet, and they would not arrive for work until sunrise (*Bava Metzia* 83b).

15. וַיָּמָד שֵׁשׁ־שְׂעֹרִים — *He measured out six barley stalks.*

Since he was giving her six individual stalks, why does the verse say וַיָּמָד, *he measured*? It would be more accurate to say וַיִּמְנֶה, *he counted.*

not want to redeem you, then [I swear that] as
Hashem lives, I will redeem you! Lie down until
the morning."
[14] *So she lay at his feet until the morning and*
she arose before one man could recognize another,
for he said, "Let it not be known that the woman
came to the threshing floor." [15] *And he said, "Hold*
out the shawl that is upon you and grasp it." She
held it, and he measured out barley stalks, and
set it on her; then he went to the city.
[16] *She came to her mother-in-law who said,*
"Who are you, my daughter?" So she told her all

The sense of the word is that he went through the stalks to find large ones. *Rashi* cites the Sages that Boaz alluded prophetically to her descendant David, who would have six outstanding character traits. This is based on the relationship of the word וַיָּמָד to the word מִדָּה, *character trait.*

☐ וַיָּשֶׁת עָלֶיהָ — *And set it upon her.*

The Talmud (*Avodah Zarah* 8b) speaks of the custom to plant barley before a wedding to symbolize that the bride should be fruitful and have abundant offspring, like barley growing in a field. This was the blessing Boaz wished to signify to Ruth as they parted that morning. Furthermore, by giving her six barley stalks he meant to signify his blessing that she should have six distinguished offspring, each of whom would have six blessings. The six offspring were David, Daniel, Chananyah, Mishael, Azaryah, and the future King Messiah. The blessings are enumerated in Sanhedrin 93b.

☐ וַיָּבֹא הָעִיר — *Then he went to the city.*

Boaz accompanied her until the city limits (*Midrash Rabbah*), and then he went into the city alone, with Ruth following at a discreet distance.

16. מִי־אַתְּ בִּתִּי — *"Who are you, my daughter?"*

"Are you still single or are you a married woman?" (*Midrash Rabbah*). Naomi did not mean this literally, because Ruth and Boaz could not have been actually married without witnesses. Rather Naomi meant

ג/יז־יח יז אֵת כָּל־אֲשֶׁר עָשָׂה־לָהּ הָאִישׁ: וַתֹּאמֶר
°אֵלַי ק שֵׁשׁ־הַשְּׂעֹרִים הָאֵלֶּה נָתַן לִי כִּי אָמַר °אֵלַי
[°אלי קרי ולא כתיב] אַל־תָּבוֹאִי רֵיקָם אֶל־חֲמוֹתֵךְ:
יח וַתֹּאמֶר שְׁבִי בִתִּי עַד אֲשֶׁר תֵּדְעִין אֵיךְ
יִפֹּל דָּבָר כִּי לֹא יִשְׁקֹט הָאִישׁ כִּי אִם־כִּלָּה
הַדָּבָר הַיּוֹם:

רש"י

(יח) כי אם כלה. האיש את **הדבר היום:**

---

to ask if Boaz had promised to marry her or if the issue of *yibum* was still up in the air.

☐ **כָּל־אֲשֶׁר עָשָׂה לָהּ הָאִישׁ** — *All that the man had done for her.*
Ruth explained that she would soon be a married woman because Boaz had assured her that either he or Tov would marry her.

17. שֵׁשׁ־הַשְּׂעֹרִים — *The six barley stalks,*
which Boaz had given her as an omen that she would have many offspring.

☐ **כִּי אָמַר** — *Because he said.*
The text is read as though the unwritten word אֵלַי, *to me,* appears in

that the man had done for her, [17] *and she said,*
"He gave me these six barley stalks because he said to me, 'Do not go empty-handed to your mother-in-law.' "
[18] *Then she said, "Sit [patiently], my daughter,*
until you know how the matter will turn out, for the man will not rest unless he settles the matter today."

---

the verse. This word would imply that Ruth's bright future would be in her own merit, but she omitted this word when she related the events to Naomi. In her great sensitivity, Ruth wanted to make it sound as if all these good tidings were because of Naomi and to her credit.

18. אֵיךְ יִפֹּל דָּבָר — *How the matter will turn out,*
i.e., whether Ruth would be married to Boaz or to Tov.

□ כִּי אִם־כִּלָּה הַדָּבָר הַיּוֹם — *Unless he settles the matter today.*
Although it was not such an emergency that it could not wait a few days, Naomi was sure that Boaz would never let an untrue word cross his lips. Since he had said that the matter would be settled in the morning, he will not delay. The matter would surely be concluded that very day.

א וּבֹעַז עָלָה הַשַּׁעַר וַיֵּשֶׁב שָׁם וְהִנֵּה הַגֹּאֵל
עֹבֵר אֲשֶׁר דִּבֶּר־בֹּעַז וַיֹּאמֶר סוּרָה שְׁבָה־
ב פֹּה פְּלֹנִי אַלְמֹנִי וַיָּסַר וַיֵּשֵׁב: וַיִּקַּח עֲשָׂרָה
אֲנָשִׁים מִזִּקְנֵי הָעִיר וַיֹּאמֶר שְׁבוּ־פֹה
ג וַיֵּשֵׁבוּ: וַיֹּאמֶר לַגֹּאֵל חֶלְקַת הַשָּׂדֶה
אֲשֶׁר לְאָחִינוּ לֶאֱלִימֶלֶךְ מָכְרָה נָעֳמִי

רש"י

ד (א) פלני אלמוני. ולא נכתב שמו לפי שלא אבה לגאול: **פלני אלמני.** מתורגם בנביאים (שמואל-א כא, ג) כסי וטמיר: **פלני.** מכוסה ונעלם, לשון (דברים יז, ח) כי יפלא, (בראשית יח, יד) היפלא מה' דבר: **אלמני.** אלמון מבלי שם. (ס"א אלמוני שהיה אלמן מד"ת, שהיה לו לדרוש עמוני ולא עמונית מואבי ולא מואבית והוא אמר פן אשחית את נחלתי):

Chapter 4

1. **עָלָה הַשַּׁעַר** — *Had gone up to the gate.*

Boaz wanted to publicize the relatively unknown law that a female Moabite convert was permitted to marry a Jew. The place to do that was in a *beis din*. Throuhout Scripture, we find that the courts would customarily sit near the city gate (e.g., *Devarim* 22:15), so Boaz now went to the gate, where he would present the case to the *beis din*.

☐ **הַגֹּאֵל עֹבֵר** — *The redeemer . . . passed by.*

Boaz had intended to summon the redeemer to the court, but now that was unnecessary, since the redeemer had come to the gate.

☐ **סוּרָה שְׁבָה־פֹּה** — *Come over, sit down here.*

The redeemer was not part of the *beis din*, nor, as we shall see below, was he qualified to be. Therefore, Boaz had to invite him to come to the court so that they could discuss and adjudicate the matter.

☐ **פְּלֹנִי אַלְמֹנִי** — *Ploni Almoni.*

According to one view in the Midrash, this was his name; accordingly the man must have had two names, since Boaz had previously referred to him as Tov. Another view is that *Ploni Almoni* is a description, rather than a name. We interpret the name according to the latter opinion, as follows:

1 *Boaz, meanwhile, had gone up to the gate,*
and sat down there. Just then, the redeemer of
whom Boaz had spoken passed by. He said,
"Come over, sit down here, Ploni Almoni," and
he came over and sat down. 2 *Then he took ten*
men of the elders of the city, and said, "Sit
here," and they sat down.
3 *Then he said to the redeemer, "The parcel of*
land which belonged to our brother, Elimelech,
is being offered for sale by Naomi who has

The word *Ploni* is related to כִּי יִפָּלֵא מִמְּךָ דָבָר לַמִּשְׁפָּט, *If a matter of judgment is* **hidden** *from you* (*Devarim* 17:8). Here, the law of a Moabite woman *was hidden* from the redeemer. And he was *Almoni*, from the word אַלְמָן, *widower*, in that the Torah is the "bride" of every Jew, but Tov, in his ignorance of the law, was a "widower" from the Torah, as it were.

2. וַיִּקַּח עֲשָׂרָה אֲנָשִׁים — *Then he took ten men.*

The verse does not say וַיָּסַר, *he took aside*, which would imply that the ten men were not part of the *beis din*. Rather they were members of the court and Boaz now asked them to convene for two reasons: to publicize the law that Ruth was permitted to marry a Jew, and so that there would be a *minyan* for the wedding.

3. מָכְרָה נָעֳמִי — *Is being offered for sale by Naomi.*

Naomi could not actually "sell" the field because, under the laws of inheritance, the property of Elimelech went to his sons, and after their death it went to the next closest heirs, who were respectively Tov, Boaz, and Naomi (unless she had a brother, who would have priority over her). However, under the terms of her *kesubah*, Naomi had a lien on the field, and she was entitled to demand that it be sold and the proceeds be used to satisfy her *kesubah*. It is clear that she had not actually sold her claim to the property, because verse 5 speaks of buying the field from her. The reason our verse speaks of her wishing to sell the field is because she, as a widow, had a right to remain in the field in payment for her *kesubah*, and the redeemer could buy the right from her in payment of her *kesubah*.

ד/ד־ה

ד הַשָּׁבָה מִשְּׂדֵה מוֹאָב: וַאֲנִי אָמַרְתִּי אֶגְלֶה
אָזְנְךָ לֵאמֹר קְנֵה נֶגֶד הַיֹּשְׁבִים וְנֶגֶד זִקְנֵי
עַמִּי אִם־תִּגְאַל גְּאָל וְאִם־לֹא יִגְאַל הַגִּידָה
לִּי ואדע כִּי אֵין זוּלָתְךָ לִגְאוֹל וְאָנֹכִי — וְאֵדְעָה ק׳
ה אַחֲרֶיךָ וַיֹּאמֶר אָנֹכִי אֶגְאָל: וַיֹּאמֶר בֹּעַז
בְּיוֹם־קְנוֹתְךָ הַשָּׂדֶה מִיַּד נָעֳמִי וּמֵאֵת רוּת
הַמּוֹאֲבִיָּה אֵשֶׁת־הַמֵּת קָנִיתָ [קניתי כ׳]

רש״י

(ד) ואדעה כי אין זולתך. קרוב לגאול: **(ה) ומאת רות המואביה.** אתה צריך לקנות והיא אינה מתרצה אלא אם כן תשאנה:

☐ **הַשָּׁבָה מִשְּׂדֵה מוֹאָב** — *Who has returned from the fields of Moab.*

Boaz added this fact to foreclose the possible argument that by letting years go by without trying to collect her *kesubah*, Naomi had, in effect, waived her right to the *kesubah*. Such an argument would be wrong on two counts: since she was in Moab, she could not claim the *kesubah;* and the halachah is that a woman is entitled to payment even after an interval longer than ten years.

4. **אֶגְלֶה אָזְנְךָ** — *I shall inform you,*

i.e., I would tell you everything involved in your responsibility to redeem, including the request that you marry Ruth. Boaz went on to make clear in unmistakable terms that he was not holding back any information: that Tov had the first right of refusal to both redeem the property and marry Ruth, and that Boaz was ready to do both if Tov refused.

☐ **וְאִם־לֹא יִגְאַל** — *And if he will not redeem.*

Here Boaz changed from second person to third person. Until now he was speaking directly to Tov; now he addressed the court.

☐ **וְאֵדְעָה** — *That I may know.*

The *hei* [ה] at the end of the word is not written, but it is pronounced in the reading. The letter with a dot [ה] indicates that the word can be rendered *I will know* **her**. Thus Boaz was intimating that if Tov refused, he, Boaz, would marry Ruth.

returned from the fields of Moab. [4] *I resolved that I*
shall inform you to this effect: Buy it in the
presence of those sitting here and in the presence
of the elders of my people. If you are willing to
redeem, redeem! And if he will not redeem, tell
me, that I may know; for there is no one else to
redeem but you, and I am after you." And he
said, "I am willing to redeem."
[5] *Then Boaz said, "The day you buy the field*
from the hand of Naomi, you must also buy it
from Ruth the Moabite, wife of the deceased, to

☐ אֵין זוּלָתְךָ לִגְאוֹל — *There is no one else to redeem but you,* i.e., there is no relative as close as you. Tov was Elimelech's brother, while Boaz was only a nephew.

5. מִיַּד נָעֳמִי —*From the hand of Naomi.*

To compensate her for her *kesubah,* Tov would have to give her money for the field. But Boaz also added that Tov would have to compensate Ruth. Even though she was not a Jewess when she was married to Machlon, and therefore the halachic requirement of a *kesubah* did not apply to her, Machlon had voluntarily undertaken the responsibility of a *kesubah.* Ruth would not release Tov from this debt unless he married her, for her interest was not to get money but to have a Jewish marriage. She was prepared to allow any *kesubah* payments to go to Naomi.

One may wonder why Tov could not simply have given her payment for the *kesubah* and be free of any further claim. It may be that since she was a Moabite princess, Machlon had obligated himself to a much larger financial settlement than the field was worth. For example, if instead of the minimum 200-zuz amount of the *kesubah*, Machlon had promised Ruth a thousand zuz. Theoretically Ruth could have argued that the field was worth a thousand zuz to her and she would not surrender her claim for less — unless Tov agreed to marry her, in which case she would give up her lien free of charge. That, Tov was not willing to do.

ו לְהָקִים שֵׁם־הַמֵּת עַל־נַחֲלָתוֹ: וַיֹּאמֶר
הַגֹּאֵל לֹא אוּכַל °לגאול לִי פֶּן־אַשְׁחִית
אֶת־נַחֲלָתִי גְּאַל־לְךָ אַתָּה אֶת־גְּאֻלָּתִי כִּי
ז לֹא־אוּכַל לִגְאֹול: וְזֹאת לְפָנִים בְּיִשְׂרָאֵל
עַל־הַגְּאוּלָּה וְעַל־הַתְּמוּרָה לְקַיֵּם כָּל־דָּבָר

°לִגְאָל־ ק׳

רש"י

(ו) **פן אשחית את נחלתי.** זרעי, כמו (תהלים קכז, ג) נחלת ה' בנים, לתת פגם בזרעי, שנאמר (דברים כג, ד) לא יבא עמוני ומואבי, וטעה בעמוני ולא עמונית: (ז) **על הגאלה.** זו מכירה: **תמורה.** זו חליפין:

☐ **לְהָקִים שֵׁם־הַמֵּת** — *To perpetuate the name of the deceased.*

As long as Machlon's widow would live on his land, people would remember Machlon and his memory would survive. One may wonder why anyone would want the name of Machlon to be remembered as the one who married a non-Jewish woman; such a memory would disgrace, not honor him. It may be that most people thought that Ruth had converted before Machlon married her.

Another difficulty: Why couldn't Tov say that he would redeem the portions of the field that Naomi and her other son Kilion were entitled to, and leave Ruth with the rest of the field? Perhaps he could indeed have done so, but either those two portions of the field were not economically feasible, or Ruth's portion, based on her marital agreement with Machlon, was the major part of the field, and it was not worth Tov's while to buy the rest of the property.

6. לֹא־אוּכַל — *Then I cannot.*

Tov was under the impression — as most people were up to then — that the prohibition against marriage with Moabite converts applied to women as well as to men, and therefore he could not marry Ruth. It would seem that it would have been more accurate for Tov to say "*I **may** not,*" meaning that it was halachically forbidden. "I *cannot*" implies that it would be physically impossible for him to live with Ruth, which was not the case. However, the Torah often speaks of sin in terms of לֹא תוּכַל, *you cannot* (see, for example, *Devarim* 12:17), since ideally a

perpetuate the name of the deceased on his
inheritance." 6 *The redeemer said, "Then I cannot*
redeem for myself, lest I imperil my heritage. Take
over my redemption responsibility on yourself for I
am unable to redeem."
7 *Formerly this was done in Israel in cases of*
redemption and exchange transactions to validate

---

person should feel that he is physically incapable of transgressing God's will.

☐ **לִגְאָל־לִי** — *Redeem for myself.*

The word לִי, *for myself,* like the word לוֹ, *for himself* (see *Bereishis* 2:18), alludes to the marital relationship. Thus, Tov was saying that if redemption meant that he had to marry Ruth, he could not do it.

☐ **פֶּן־אַשְׁחִית אֶת־נַחֲלָתִי** — *Lest I imperil my heritage.*

Tov was referring to his future children, which are referred to as one's *heritage,* as in the verse הִנֵּה נַחֲלַת ה׳ בָּנִים, *Behold! the heritage of Hashem is children* (*Tehillim* 127:3). Tov also said that even if Boaz was right about the halachah, any offspring of Ruth would suffer from attacks on his legitimacy, as David was indeed constantly reviled by Doeg the Edomite (see *Yevamos* 76b).

7. עַל־הַגְּאֻלָּה — *In cases of redemption,*

i.e., in cases where the buyer had given the seller the right to redeem his property after the sale.

☐ **וְעַל־הַתְּמוּרָה** — *And exchange transactions.*

This refers to exchanges of one property for another. In all such cases, including redemptions, where land is involved, there must be a קִנְיָן, an act symbolizing ownership, such as the one described later in this verse. In the case of purchases or exchanges of movable items, the act described here is unnecessary; the new owner simply picks up the item or has it placed in his property. However, if one wishes to reinforce his acquisition of a movable item so that neither party can withdraw from the transaction, one may also perform the act mentioned here.

שָׁלַ֥ף אִ֛ישׁ נַעֲל֖וֹ וְנָתַ֣ן לְרֵעֵ֑הוּ וְזֹ֥את הַתְּעוּדָ֖ה
ח בְּיִשְׂרָאֵֽל׃ וַיֹּ֧אמֶר הַגֹּאֵ֛ל לְבֹ֖עַז קְנֵה־לָ֑ךְ
ט וַיִּשְׁלֹ֖ף נַעֲלֽוֹ׃ וַיֹּאמֶר֩ בֹּ֨עַז לַזְּקֵנִ֜ים וְכָל־הָעָ֗ם
עֵדִ֤ים אַתֶּם֙ הַיּ֔וֹם כִּ֤י קָנִ֙יתִי֙ אֶת־כָּל־אֲשֶׁ֣ר
לֶֽאֱלִימֶ֔לֶךְ וְאֵ֛ת כָּל־אֲשֶׁ֥ר לְכִלְי֖וֹן וּמַחְל֑וֹן
י מִיַּ֖ד נָעֳמִֽי׃ וְגַ֣ם אֶת־ר֣וּת הַמֹּאֲבִיָּה֩ אֵ֨שֶׁת
מַחְל֜וֹן קָנִ֧יתִי לִ֣י לְאִשָּׁ֗ה לְהָקִ֤ים שֵׁם־הַמֵּת֙
עַל־נַחֲלָת֔וֹ וְלֹֽא־יִכָּרֵ֧ת שֵׁם־הַמֵּ֛ת מֵעִ֥ם
אֶחָ֖יו וּמִשַּׁ֣עַר מְקוֹמ֑וֹ עֵדִ֥ים אַתֶּ֖ם הַיּֽוֹם׃

רש"י

שלף איש נעלו. זהו קניין כמו שאנו קונין בסודר במקום נעל. ורבותינו ז"ל (בבא מציעא מז, א) נחלקו בדבר מי נתן למי, יש אומרים קונין בכליו של קונה ובועז נתן לגואל, ויש אומרים קונין בכליו של מקנה וגואל נתן לבועז: **וזאת התעודה בישראל.** משפט העדות: (י) **להקים שם המת על נחלתו.** מתוך שאשתו יוצאה ובאה בנחלה ומכנסת ומוציאה, אומרים זאת היתה אשת מחלון ושמו נזכר עליה:

☐ **שָׁלַף אִישׁ נַעֲלוֹ** — *One would remove his shoe*
and give it to the other party. This symbolizes a trade: in return for the shoe, the owner gives permission for the redemption of the field.

☐ **וְזֹאת הַתְּעוּדָה** — *This was the process of ratification.*
Witnesses would testify that the "trade," which obligated the parties, had been carried out.

8. **קְנֵה־לָךְ** — *Buy it for yourself.*
Having refused Boaz's demand that he marry Ruth, Tov told Boaz to buy the privilege for himself, whereupon . . .

☐ **וַיִּשְׁלֹף נַעֲלוֹ** — *He removed his shoe.*
Boaz removed his own shoe and handed it to Tov as the "exchange" that signified his acquisition of the right to redeem the field and marry Ruth.

9. **עֵדִים אַתֶּם** — *You are witnesses this day.*
The transaction did not have to be witnessed in order to be valid and binding. However Boaz wanted it to be witnessed so that Tov could not

any matter: One would remove his shoe, and give
it to the other. This was the process of ratification in
Israel. [8] *So when the redeemer said to Boaz, "Buy it*
for yourself," he removed his shoe.
[9] *And Boaz said to the elders, and to all the*
people, "You are witnesses this day, that I have
bought all that was Elimelech's and all that was
Kilion's and Machlon's from the hand of Naomi.
[10] *And also [the right to marry] Ruth the Moabite,*
the wife of Machlon, have I acquired as my wife, to
perpetuate the name of the deceased on his
inheritance, that the name of the deceased not be
cut off from among his brethren, and from the gate
of his place. You are witnesses today."

---

change his mind and come back later to claim his right as the primary redeemer.

☐ מִיַּד נָעֳמִי — *From Naomi.*

Perhaps the entire value of the field, which had been inherited by Machlon and Kilion, was needed to pay for Naomi's *kesubah*, since Naomi had a prior claim. If so, what were Ruth's rights in the field? We may surmise that Naomi voluntarily gave up her right to Machlon's share so that Ruth could collect it for her own *kesubah*. Thus, although Ruth forgave payment of her *kesubah* in favor of Naomi, Naomi did not want to accept the benefit.

10. וְגַם אֶת־רוּת . . . קָנִיתִי — *And also [the right to marry] Ruth . . . have I acquired.*

It was important for Boaz to specify that this right of *yibum* was part of the transaction. If there had been an implication that purchase involved only the field, Tov could have claimed that his waiver was erroneous and therefore not binding, because he was willing to purchase the property; he objected only to marrying Ruth.

☐ עֵדִים אַתֶּם הַיּוֹם — *You are witnesses today.*

In the previous verse, they were witnessing a transaction. Now Boaz was calling upon the court to be witnesses to something else. By

יא וַיֹּאמְרוּ כָּל־הָעָם אֲשֶׁר־בַּשַּׁעַר וְהַזְּקֵנִים
עֵדִים יִתֵּן יהוה אֶת־הָאִשָּׁה הַבָּאָה אֶל־
בֵּיתֶךָ כְּרָחֵל ׀ וּכְלֵאָה אֲשֶׁר בָּנוּ שְׁתֵּיהֶם
אֶת־בֵּית יִשְׂרָאֵל וַעֲשֵׂה־חַיִל בְּאֶפְרָתָה
יב וּקְרָא־שֵׁם בְּבֵית לָחֶם: וִיהִי בֵיתְךָ כְּבֵית
פֶּרֶץ אֲשֶׁר־יָלְדָה תָמָר לִיהוּדָה מִן־הַזֶּרַע

רש"י

(יא) כרחל וכלאה. אף על פי שהיו משבט יהודה ומבני לאה, מודים הם על רחל שהיתה עיקרה של בית, והקדימו רחל ללאה: **וקרא שם.** כלומר יגדל שמך: **(יב) כבית פרץ.** שיצאנו ממנו:

---

proclaiming that he was about to marry Ruth, Boaz was stating the law that was not commonly known, that a Jew is permitted to marry a female convert from Moab. He wanted this to be publicized so that their future offspring would not be stigmatized as children of a non-halachic marriage, and that this be remembered permanently so that their lineage would never be questioned.

11. עֵדִים — *"We are witnesses!"*

The court agreed to proclaim that it had witnessed and agreed with the halachah as Boaz had explained it.

☐ **יִתֵּן ה׳ אֶת־הָאִשָּׁה... כְּרָחֵל וּכְלֵאָה** — *May HASHEM make the woman... like Rachel and like Leah.*

May Ruth be the mother of kings, like Rachel and Leah: Saul and the kings of the Ten Tribes descended from Rachel, and the Davidic dynasty from Leah.

☐ **אֲשֶׁר בָּנוּ שְׁתֵּיהֶם** — *Both of whom built.*

Rachel and Leah were the mainstays of Jacob's family. The word שְׁתֵּיהֶם is an unusual blend of male and female: שְׁתֵּי is feminine, but the *mem* at the end the word is masculine. The implication is that since Rachel and Leah built the family of Jacob, they were equal to him and could be described in the masculine gender.

☐ **אֶת־בֵּית יִשְׂרָאֵל** — *The House of Israel.*

Thanks to them, Jacob was able to leave Charan. Had they not

11 *Then all the people who were at the gate, and*
the elders, said, "[We are] witnesses! May Hashem
make the woman who is coming into your house
like Rachel and like Leah, both of whom built the
House of Israel. May you prosper in Ephrath and be
famous in Bethlehem; 12 *and may your house be*
like the house of Peretz whom Tamar bore to Judah,

---

encouraged Jacob to leave the house of Laban, it would have been difficult for him to take his family to *Eretz Yisrael.*

☐ וַעֲשֵׂה־חַיִל — *May you prosper.*

The numerical value of חַיִל is 48, which alludes to the forty-eight traits through which a person acquires Torah knowledge (*Avos* 6:5). Thus the people blessed Ruth that her offspring should become great Torah scholars.

☐ בְּאֶפְרָתָה — *In Ephrath.*

Ephrath was another name of Miriam, the sister of Moses. When she and her mother, Yocheved, defied Pharaoh and saved the Jewish baby boys, God gave them a blessing that royal dynasties should descend from them. Now the people blessed Ruth that she should share in that blessing.

☐ שֵׁם — *And be famous.*

In this context, to proclaim her "*name*" is to wish her great success in a prestigious undertaking, which will give her an excellent reputation.

12. וִיהִי בֵיתְךָ כְּבֵית פֶּרֶץ — *And may your house be like the house of Peretz.*

Peretz was the son of Judah who was destined to become the ancestor of Israel's royal family. Boaz and Tov were both descendants of Peretz (see vs. 19-21). The onlookers wished Boaz that Ruth and he — rather than Tov, who had passed up the opportunity to marry Ruth — would have a child who will be destined for the throne.

☐ אֲשֶׁר־יָלְדָה תָמָר לִיהוּדָה — *Whom Tamar bore to Judah.*

The well-wishers alluded to a handicap that they prayed Boaz and Ruth would overcome. When Tamar became pregnant by Judah, it was an event that opened them to humiliating criticism (see *Bereishis* 38:13-30). Just as Tamar was derided as an inappropriate match for a

יג אֲשֶׁר יִתֵּן יהוה לְךָ מִן־הַנַּעֲרָה הַזֹּאת: וַיִּקַּח
בֹּעַז אֶת־רוּת וַתְּהִי־לוֹ לְאִשָּׁה וַיָּבֹא אֵלֶיהָ
יד וַיִּתֵּן יהוה לָהּ הֵרָיוֹן וַתֵּלֶד בֵּן: וַתֹּאמַרְנָה
הַנָּשִׁים אֶל־נָעֳמִי בָּרוּךְ יהוה אֲשֶׁר לֹא
הִשְׁבִּית לָךְ גֹּאֵל הַיּוֹם וְיִקָּרֵא שְׁמוֹ
טו בְּיִשְׂרָאֵל: וְהָיָה לָךְ לְמֵשִׁיב נֶפֶשׁ וּלְכַלְכֵּל
אֶת־שֵׂיבָתֵךְ כִּי כַלָּתֵךְ אֲשֶׁר־אֲהֵבַתֶךְ
יְלָדַתּוּ אֲשֶׁר־הִיא טוֹבָה לָךְ מִשִּׁבְעָה בָּנִים:

---

son of Jacob, so Ruth was derided as an inappropriate match for the Judge of the Jewish people. Indeed the Talmud (*Yoma* 22b) states that it is good for a leader to have קוּפָּה שֶׁל שְׁרָצִים תְּלוּיָה לוֹ מֵאֲחוֹרָיו, *a box of vermin suspended behind him*, i.e., criticism of his lineage so that he should not become arrogant. Now, therefore, when Boaz and Ruth were suffring from such criticism, the people blessed them that just as Judah and Tamar persevered and earned everyone's respect, so should Boaz and Ruth be recognized and respected.

☐ **מִן־הַזֶּרַע אֲשֶׁר יִתֵּן ה׳ לְךָ מִן־הַנַּעֲרָה הַזֹּאת** — *Through the offspring which HASHEM will give you by this young woman.*

This phrase seems to imply that Boaz had offspring from his many other children. Although all his many children died in his lifetime, he apparently had grandchildren. Now the people wished him that he have a new family with *this young woman*, even though people like Tov were critical of anyone who would marry her.

13. וַיִּתֵּן ה׳ לָהּ הֵרָיוֹן — *HASHEM let her conceive.*

The blessing of the elders was beginning to be fulfilled. She conceived and gave birth to the boy who would become a link in the chain that would lead to the birth of King David.

14. אֲשֶׁר לֹא הִשְׁבִּית לָךְ גֹּאֵל — *Who has not left you without a redeemer.*

The joyous blessing of the women was that Naomi's son Machlon would now be remembered, for people would say that Machlon's wife gave birth to a son, who was the heir of Boaz.

through the offspring which Hashem will give you
by this young woman."
[13] *And so, Boaz took Ruth and she became his*
wife; and he came to her. Hashem let her conceive,
and she bore a son. [14] *And the women said to*
Naomi, "Blessed is Hashem Who has not left you
without a redeemer today! May his name be famous
in Israel. [15] *He will become your life-restorer, and to*
sustain your old age; for your daughter-in-law, who
loves you, has borne him, and she is better to you
than seven sons."

□ **הַיּוֹם** — *Today!*

Although the immediate joy was that *today* Naomi had the joy of seeing a redeemer who would perpetuate the name of her family, there would be a much more far-reaching result from this birth, because . . .

□ **וְיִקָּרֵא שְׁמוֹ בְּיִשְׂרָאֵל** — *May his name be famous in Israel.*

The name of this child will go down in history, because everyone will know that the royal family of Israel descended from Ruth, the wife of Machlon.

15. וְהָיָה לָךְ לְמֵשִׁיב נֶפֶשׁ — *He will become your life-restorer.*

He will restore the lost name of Machlon.

□ **וּלְכַלְכֵּל אֶת־שֵׂיבָתֵךְ** — *And to sustain your old age.*

The child will become the one who will take responsibility for you when you can no longer support yourself — in the Talmudic figure of speech, he will be *the cane for your hand*. The reason you will be able to rely on him is because he is the son of . . .

□ **כַּלָּתֵךְ אֲשֶׁר־אֲהֵבָתֶךְ** — *Your daughter-in-law, who loves you.*

Ruth showed her love for you by remaining with you when there seemed to be no logical reason for her not to go back to her prestigious home in Moab.

□ **מִשִּׁבְעָה בָּנִים** — *Than seven sons.*

Counting from Peretz, Boaz was the seventh generation. King David could have descended from any one of Peretz's offspring, and not from

טז וַתִּקַּח נָעֳמִי אֶת־הַיֶּלֶד וַתְּשִׁתֵהוּ בְחֵיקָהּ
יז וַתְּהִי־לוֹ לְאֹמֶנֶת: וַתִּקְרֶאנָה לוֹ הַשְּׁכֵנוֹת
שֵׁם לֵאמֹר יֻלַּד־בֵּן לְנָעֳמִי וַתִּקְרֶאנָה
שְׁמוֹ עוֹבֵד הוּא אֲבִי־יִשַׁי אֲבִי דָוִד:
יח וְאֵלֶּה תּוֹלְדוֹת פָּרֶץ פֶּרֶץ הוֹלִיד אֶת־
יט חֶצְרוֹן: וְחֶצְרוֹן הוֹלִיד אֶת־רָם וְרָם
כ הוֹלִיד אֶת־עַמִּינָדָב: וְעַמִּינָדָב הוֹלִיד
אֶת־נַחְשׁוֹן וְנַחְשׁוֹן הוֹלִיד אֶת־שַׂלְמָה:

רש"י

(יח) ואלה תולדות פרץ. לפי שייחס את דוד על שמה של רות המואביה, חזר וייחסו על שם יהודה:

חסלת מגלת רות:

Boaz. However, because Boaz married Ruth, he merited that the royal family of Israel should descend from Oved, the son they had together. Because Boaz was so righteous, he, not Tov, had the privilege of marrying Ruth.

16. וַתְּהִי־לוֹ לְאֹמֶנֶת — *And she became his nurse.*

Naomi cared for the baby and supervised his upbringing and education.

17. יֻלַּד־בֵּן לְנָעֳמִי — *"A son was born to Naomi."*

As the Talmud says, one who teaches Torah to the son of his fellow is regarded as if he had given birth to the son. Thus, Naomi, who undertook responsibility for Oved's Torah education, could legitimately be called the one who gave birth to him.

☐ **עוֹבֵד** — *Oved.*

The name means *"One Who Serves."* Naomi and her companions gave him this name to signify their expectation that he would dedicate himself to serve the people — not like Elimelech, Machlon, and Kilion, who deserted *Eretz Yisrael* when the people faced a crisis. The verse refers to Oved as the father and grandfather of Yishai and David to imply that the blessed sense of mission implied by his name carried over to his offspring.

[16] *Naomi took the child, and held it in her bosom, and she became his nurse.* [17] *The neighborhood women gave him a name, saying, "A son is born to Naomi." They named him Oved; he was the father of Yishai, the father of David.*

[18] *And these are the generations of Peretz: Peretz begot Chetzron;* [19] *and Chetzron begot Ram, and Ram begot Aminadav;* [20] *and Aminadav begot Nachshon, and Nachshon begot Salmah;*

☐ אֲבִי־יִשַׁי — *The father of Yishai,*

who served many people by teaching them Torah.

☐ אֲבִי דָוִד — *The father of David,*

who was a fitting grandson of Oved, the *Servant*. David would be the loyal and dedicated servant of Hashem and of the Jewish people.

18. וְאֵלֶּה — *And these are.*

The conjunctive *vav* connects this genealogy to the narrative above. Everything that happened in the story of Ruth and Naomi was so that the royal destiny of Peretz be realized.

19. חֶצְרוֹן — *Chetzron.*

He is named among those who came to Egypt with Yaakov (*Bereishis* 46:12) in the year 2237. Chetzron's son was Ram, whose son was Aminadav, both of whom were born during the 210 years that the Jewish people were in Egypt. Aharon HaKohen married Aminadav's daughter in Egypt.

20. נַחְשׁוֹן — *Nachshon.*

He, too, was born in Egypt, since he was the leader of the tribe of Judah during Israel's second year in the Wilderness. He died during that year (*Seder Olam*)

☐ שַׂלְמָה —*Salmah.*

Salmah, also known as Salmon (next verse), was able to enter *Eretz Yisrael,* so he had to be less than twenty years old when the Spies broke the spirit and faith of the people and caused the decree that everyone over the age of twenty would die in the Wilderness. That decree was issued in the second year after the Exodus, so either Salmah was

כא וְשַׂלְמוֹן הוֹלִיד אֶת־בֹּעַז וּבֹעַז הוֹלִיד אֶת־
כב עוֹבֵד: וְעֹבֵד הוֹלִיד אֶת־יִשָׁי וְיִשַׁי הוֹלִיד
אֶת־דָּוִד:

סכום פסוקי דספר רות שמונים וחמשה
וסימנו סורה שבה **פה** פלוני אלמני. **ובעז** הוליד את עובד סימן.
וחציו ותאמר רות המואביה גם כי אמר אלי. וסדרו אחד.

---

nineteen years old or younger when the Jews left Egypt, or else he was born in the Wilderness.

21. וְשַׂלְמוֹן הוֹלִיד אֶת־בֹּעַז — *And Salmon begot Boaz.*

Since Boaz died 309 years after the nation entered *Eretz Yisrael*, there was, remarkably, a span of at least 348 years from the birth of Salmah to the death of his son Boaz. (This assumes that Salmah was born during the Jews' second year in the Wilderness, which is when his father, Nachshon, passed away. If Salmah was 19 when the Jews left Egypt, the time-span was 367 years!)

☐ **וּבֹעַז הוֹלִיד אֶת־עוֹבֵד** — *And Boaz begot Oved.*

This was in the year 2,797 from Creation.

22. וְיִשַׁי הוֹלִיד אֶת־דָּוִד — *And Yishai begot David.*

David was born in the year 2854 from Creation.

The following is a chronology of the seven generations:

[] **Peretz** was born in 2229, 9 years before Yaakov and his family descended to Egypt (*Seder Olam* 3).

[21] *and Salman begot Boaz, and Boaz begot*
Oved; [22] *and Oved begot Yishai, and Yishai begot*
David.

[] **Chetzron** was born in 2237, one year before the descent to Egypt (ibid.).

[] **Ram, Aminadav,** and **Nachshon** were born in Egypt. Nachshon died in the second year after the Exodus from Egypt (*Seder Olam* 12).

[] **Salmon** may have been born during the first two years after the Exodus, or else he was born in Egypt, but was less than 19 years old at the time of the Exodus.

[] **Boaz** died in 2797, and **Oved** was born in the same year (*Gra* to *Seder Olam*).

[] **Yishai** was born during the 57 years between Oved's birth and David's birth. The exact year is not known.

[] **David** was born in 2854 and died in 2924.

The construction of the Beis Hamikdash was begun four years after David's death, in 2928, and was completed in 2935 (*I Melachim* 6:1,38).

Epilogue

אָמַר רַב זְעִירָא, מְגִלָּה זוֹ אֵין בָּהּ לֹא טֻמְאָה וְלֹא טַהֲרָה, לֹא אִסּוּר וְלֹא הֶתֵּר, וְלָמָּה נִכְתְּבָה? לְלַמֶּדְךָ כַּמָּה שָׂכָר טוֹב לְגוֹמְלֵי חֲסָדִים.

Rav Zeira said: This scroll [of Ruth contains neither [laws of] ritual impurity or purity, nor what is forbidden or permitted, so why was it written? To teach you the great reward of those who perform deeds of kindness (*Rus Rabbah* 2:14).

This Midrash speaks of Ruth and Boaz, both of whom performed extraordinary acts of kindness. Ruth's generosity to her mother-in-law was known and admired throughout Bethlehem (see 2:11), in not abandoning her even though she, Ruth, knew that her prospects as a poor convert were bleak. Nevertheless, she set aside all such considerations in order to help the widowed and lonely Naomi. Her marriage to the much older Boaz in order to keep alive the memory of her late husband, Machlon, was also widely admired as a kind deed (3:10). Her reward was very great. She became the "Mother of Royalty," as the ancestress of King David. In blessing her, Boaz alluded to a further element of her reward. He said, וּתְהִי מַשְׂכֻּרְתֵּךְ שְׁלֵמָה מֵעִם ה׳, *may your payment be full from HASHEM* (2:12). The word שְׁלֵמָה can also be pronounced שְׁלֹמֹה, *Shlomo*, or King Solomon, son of David and descendant of Ruth. The Sages teach that Ruth lived so long that she saw Solomon on the throne of Israel (*Bava Basra* 91b).

As for Boaz, his greatest act of kindness was marrying Ruth, in order to keep alive the memory of Machlon, even though he was not Machlon's brother and therefore the commandment of יִבּוּם, *levirate marriage*, did not apply to him. Boaz at that time was elderly and, in fact, he died the day after he consummated his marriage with Ruth and she conceived. Thus, their child was called a son of Naomi and the property that Boaz redeemed was thought of by the people as that of Naomi's child. Consequently, Boaz's act was entirely unselfish; it was an act of pure kindness.

Such kindness was a necessary component of *Malchus*, Jewish royalty, because the king must understand that he is God's representative to rule His people with kindness and generosity. Because David embodied such kindness and demonstrated it as a shepherd he was chosen to be king, as we are told: וַיִּבְחַר בְּדָוִד עַבְדּוֹ וַיִּקָּחֵהוּ מִמִּכְלְאֹת צֹאן, *And He chose David, His servant, and took him from the sheep corrals* (*Tehillim* 78:70). Just as a shepherd is devoted to the welfare of his flock, so must a Jewish leader be dedicated to the welfare of his people. He must see himself as a servant of the public, and must remember that he ascended to the throne only because of his great-grandfather and great-grandmother.

The Sages (*Succah* 21b) teach אֲפִילּוּ שִׂיחַת חוּלִּין שֶׁל תַּלְמִידֵי חֲכָמִים צְרִיכָה לִמּוּד, *Even the casual conversation of Torah scholars merits study*. How much more so is the Book of Ruth, written by the prophet Samuel, eminently worthy of study as it has much to teach us. True, it may be said that the primary purpose of the Book is to teach the lineage of the Davidic dynasty, but there is surely much more. Although the Book seems to be a simple narrative, it is the source of many teachings, both ethical and legal, as follows:

1. The Book of Ruth begins by saying that there was a famine in the Land, and because of it, Elimelech took his family to Moab, where he and his two sons died. The Sages (*Bava Basra* 91a) teach that they were punished for deserting *Eretz Yisrael* at a time when their fellow Jews were in need. Of course, there are conditions under which it is permitted to leave the Holy Land and this is not the place to discuss these laws, and whether the prohibition applies after the destruction of the Beis Hamikdash. However, it is clear that one should not leave *Eretz Yisrael* without a good reason (ibid. 91b). Another aspect of their sin is that they did not pray for their hungry

brethren. They cared only about their own welfare, and for that they deserved to be punished. As the Sages teach (*Taanis* 11a), when the community is suffering, one has no right to ignore it in favor of one's own personal convenience or comfort.

2. Jews do not proselytize. In fact, someone who wishes to convert should be discouraged at first, until it is clear that his motive is sincere and that he is not doing so for personal benefit. We see this from Naomi, who urged her daughters-in-law to return to their Moabite families, rather than convert to Judaism.

3. However, if it is clear that the potential convert is sincere, he should no longer be discouraged. To the contrary, under such circumstances, it is a *mitzvah* to encourage him and help him join the Jewish people (*Yevamos* 47b). This, too, is derived from Naomi. When it was clear that Ruth was determined to convert, despite the difficulties that she knew would await her, Naomi welcomed her decision.

4. When Ruth went to find a field where she could glean food for herself and Naomi, she was careful about the place she chose. As the Sages (*Shabbos* 113b) teach, שֶׁהָלְכָה וּבָאת הָלְכָה וּבָאת עַד שֶׁמָּצְאָה בְּנֵי אָדָם הַמְהוּגָּנִין, *She went to and fro until she came upon decent people [working in the field]. Rashi* explains that she sought out workers who treated male and female gleaners respectfully. The lesson is that one should not associate with people who do not behave properly.

5. Boaz greeted his workers saying ה׳ עִמָּכֶם, *HASHEM be with you* (2:4). From this the Sages (*Berachos* 54a) derived: שֶׁיְּהֵא אָדָם שׁוֹאֵל אֶת שְׁלוֹם חֲבֵרוֹ בַּשֵּׁם, *A person should greet his fellow with a Name [of God]*. This is why we greet people by saying *Shalom aleichem*; the word Shalom is a reference to Hashem.

6. When Ruth told her mother-in-law the name of the person in whose field she gleaned, she said, שֵׁם הָאִישׁ אֲשֶׁר עָשִׂיתִי עִמּוֹ, which can be rendered, *the name of the man* **for whom** *I did . . .* (2:19), implying that she did a favor for Boaz. From this the Sages (*Bava Basra* 10a) derive that the recipient of charity does more for the giver than the giver does for the recipient.

   To illustrate this point, the Talmud (ibid.) relates that the Roman governor of *Eretz Yisrael* once challenged R' Akiva, "If your God loves the poor, why does He not provide for them?'' R' Akiva replied, "Because God wants to give us the means to merit the World to Come by helping the poor.''

7. When Ruth returned from the field of Boaz bearing an abundant amount of grain, Naomi blessed their benefactor, and then expressed thanks and blessing to God for not abandoning them. This teaches us that not only must we be thankful to those who help us, but we must also express thanks and blessing to God for His providing for us.

   In addition, besides thanking God for His kindness at that time, Naomi also thanked Him for enabling her to properly bury her husband and sons. When a person expresses thanks to God, he should also consider the many ways He has helped in the past — and express thanks for those goodnesses as well.

8. When Naomi instructed Ruth on how she should influence Boaz to marry her and redeem the property of their family, she told Ruth to wear her Shabbos clothing (see 3:3, with comm.). This teaches that when one is involved in a *shidduch,* one should wear one's best clothing, even the clothing that one otherwise wears only on Shabbos.

9. When Boaz sought the approval of the prior redeemer and the court to redeem the property and marry Ruth, he assembled ten elders (4:2). From this the Sages (*Kesubos* 7b) derive בִּרְכַּת חֲתָנִים בַּעֲשָׂרָה, *the marriage blessings require a quorum of ten.*

10. A law of the Torah that had become forgotten by many was revealed and propagated by Boaz when he made known his desire to marry Ruth. In the presence of the assembled judges, Boaz told the redeemer אֶגְלֶה אָזְנְךָ, *I should inform you* (4:4). The Sages (*Kesubos* 7b) explain that Boaz informed him of the proper interpretation of a Torah law. The Torah teaches לֹא־יָבֹא עַמּוֹנִי וּמוֹאָבִי בִּקְהַל ה׳, *An Ammonite and a Moabite may not marry into the congregation of* HASHEM (*Devarim* 23:4). Most people thought that this law applied to both men and women from those two nations, and if so it would be forbidden for a Jew to marry Ruth. But the true interpretation of the verse is מוֹאָבִי וְלֹא מוֹאָבִית, the prohibition applies only to a Moabite man, but not to a Moabite woman, and if so, Boaz and Ruth were permitted to marry.

11. One can acquire ownership of property only by taking possession of it through a קִנְיָן, an act that signifies ownership. One of these legally valid acts is קִנְיַן חֲלִיפִין, *acquisition through and exchange*, derived from the manner of the transaction between Boaz and the redeemer (see 4:7, with comm.).

The Torah is infinite and undoubtedly one can find countless other lessons in the Book of Ruth. Only in appearance is it a very simple, straightforward story. Beneath its deceptive simplicity are many lessons, both legal and moral.

The Book has 85 verses, and its mnemonic word is וּבֹעַז, *and Boaz*, which has the numerical value of 85. In order for Ruth to become the Mother of Royalty, she had to marry a descendant of Judah's son Peretz, *and Boaz* was the one who earned that privilege.

Alternatively, the privilege of becoming the ancestor of royalty belonged primarily to Ruth, not only because of her outstanding acts of kindness, but also because, as noted (see commentary to verse 2:14 and 4:12), a king had to be burdened by קוּפָּה שֶׁל שְׁרָצִים תְּלוּיָה לוֹ מֵאֲחוֹרָיו, *a box of vermin suspended behind him*, i.e., aspects of his lineage that would prevent him from becoming arrogant. Ruth's being a Moabite woman was that "box of vermin," and she was therefore an integral part of the Davidic lineage, but she had to marry a descendant of Peretz. Boaz became the "father of royalty" through marrying Ruth. Thus, the royal dynasty descended primarily from Ruth, וּבֹעַז, *and* — incidentally, as it were — *Boaz*.

This volume is part of
THE ARTSCROLL® SERIES
an ongoing project of
translations, commentaries and expositions on
Scripture, Mishnah, Talmud, Midrash, Halachah,
liturgy, history, the classic Rabbinic writings,
biographies and thought.

For a brochure of current publications
visit your local Hebrew bookseller
or contact the publisher:

Mesorah Publications, ltd

313 Regina Avenue
Rahway, New Jersey 07065
(718) 921-9000
www.artscroll.com

לזכר נשמת

אבינו מורינו עטרת ראשנו

מוהר״ר אהרן ז״ל בן־נון

בן מורינו הרב ר׳ אשר הי״ד פישמאן

ורעיתו מרת קריינדל ז״ל בת ר׳ מאיר צבי ז״ל

אשר הקדיש ימיו ושנותיו הארוכים לאהבת ישראל ציון וירושלים

עלה לארצינו הקדושה בנעוריו בשנות דחק ובהלה

לבנותה על פי תורתינו הקדושה ולהחזיר עטרת ציון ליושנה

התנהג כל ימיו עם כל אדם בכבוד באמונה ובאהבה

ומסר נפשו לעורר לבבות בני ישראל

לשוב לארצינו הקדושה ולצפות לגאולתה

והכל עשה לשם שמים בלא הנאת כבוד או פרוטה

יה״ר שבזכותו נזכה לגאולה שלימה במהרה

יחיאל מיכל ועטרה דזשייקאב ומשפחתם

שלום ושרה דזשייקאב ומשפחתם

יהושע הכהן ואביבה אברהם ומשפחתם

אשר יהודה דזשייקאב

The dedication in this ספר

is in memory of

Mr. Irwin Saks

ת.נ.צ.ב.ה

A generous donation was given to the

Mesivtha Tifereth Jerusalem

in his memory

by the

Irwin Saks Irrevocable Trust

Miami Beach, Florida

Mesivtha Tifereth Jerusalem

לעילוי נשמת

רות גולדה בת ר׳ שמריהו ורבקה ז״ל

נפטרה חג השבועות – ו׳ סיון תשנ״ט

בשנת „חן״ לחייה

מלאת חיים, חכמה, ודעת.

פעלה בחן *humor* ובכשרון.

התמסרה למשפחתה, וחנכה ילדיה בתורה

ובמעשים טובים

נהגה בחסד ובישר בהלכה בצניעות עם ה׳

ת.נ.צ.ב.ה

This volume of Megilat Ruth is dedicated to

our dear sister, Ruth Golda Schreiber (née Charles) ז״ל

whose untimely death on Shavuot 1999

has left us with a deep void in our hearts.

By

Ellen and Stanley Wasserman

אשרי תמימי דרך ההלכים בתורת ה׳

לזכר נשמת

ר׳ יצחק בן ר׳ אליהו פרגש ז״ל

נפ׳ ז׳ שבט תשנ״ג

In loving memory of

Issac Forgash

January 29, 1993

לזכר נשמת

מרת צביה בת ר׳ אשר אנשיל ע״ה

נפ׳ ב׳ ראש השנה — ב׳ תשרי תשס״א

In loving memory of

Sylvia Forgash

September 30, 2000

לעלוי נשמת

ר׳ יצחק בן ר׳ יהודה ליב ריבקין ז״ל

נפטר כ״ה שבט תשמ״ו

In loving memory of

Irving Rivkin

February 3, 1986

ולזכר נשמת

מרת פיגא בת ר׳ ישעי׳ ע״ה

נפטר כ״ט שבט תשס״ד

In loving memory of

Frances Rivkin

February 21, 2004

dedicated by

Mr. and Mrs. Jack Forgash and Family

In Memory
of our beloved parents

Jacob Seidman

ר׳ יעקב יצחק בן ר׳ נחמיה שמואל הלוי ע״ה

נפטר יא׳ תמוז תשל״ג

תנצבה

ואשתו

Malya Seidman

שיינדל מליא בת ר׳ ישעי הכהן ע״ה

נפטרה ו׳ ניסן תשמ״ד

תנצבה

Who instilled in us
love and reverence
for Torah and its Guiding Lights

Sheldon and Pearl Seidman
and Family

לזכר נשמת

ר׳ דוד בר׳ אברהם ז״ל

ר׳ שלמה זלמן בר׳ יצחק ז״ל

dedicated by

Ezra and Debbie Beyman

In Everlasting Memory of

Miriam (Manya) Suss

האשה היקרה מרים בת ר׳ חיים יוסף ע״ה

נפטרה ד׳ כסלו תשס״ו

The crown Jewel of our family
If all the heavens were parchment — if all the seas were ink
And all the forest were quills,
We could not even begin to sing her praises.

Loved by all who knew her.
Her devotion to her husband, children, grandchildren
is legend, her chesed was far reaching.

May she be an inspiration to us all.

The generation of Shomrei Torah and mitzvos
she and her loving husband raised
is her greatest tribute.

Dedicated by the

Suss, Charlap, Wolfson & Silverstein
Families

תנצבה

נר זכרון

לע״נ ידיד נאמן של מרן ראש הישיבה שליט״א

וידיד מסור לישיבה הקדושה

חכם רפאל ע״ה

בן חכם רבי חייא זצ״ל

ומלכה בת ר׳ אליהו זצ״ל

בן בנו של הדיין המצויין המפורסם

לשם ותהילה חה״ש מאור הגולה

הרב הדיין חכם רפאל אריה ס״ט זצוק״ל מקשאן־פרס.

נלב״ע במוצאי שבת קודש ד׳ שבט התשנ״ז

תנצב״ה

עד אשר יקיצו וירננו שוכני עפר

יהיה זכרו ברוך

הונצח ע״י

אשתו ובניו ובנותיו

למשפחת אריה

לזכרון נצח

We pay tribute to our Grandmothers
who passed away in Europe
before and during the war.
That we are here and that the
Torah community thrives in America
is thanks to their מסירת נפש
and the seeds they planted
and their children who nurtured them.

Moshe and Esther Beinhorn
and Family

מצבת זכרון

ר׳ אליהו ב״ר אליעזר ז״ל

נפטר כ״ח שבט

וזוגתו יעטע בת ר׳ משה הכהן ע״ה

נפטרה יו״ד כסלו

ר׳ יוסף ב״ר שמעון ז״ל

נפטר י״ג מנחם אב

וזוגתו בילה בת ר׳ אליעזר גדליה ע״ה

נפטרה ח׳ אדר

האשה רחל בת החבר יעקב ע״ה

נפטרה כ״ד חשון

הילד אליהו ב״ר יוסף שמעון ע״ה

נפטר י״ב מנחם אב

תנצב״ה

In revered honor of the Rosh Hayeshiva,

Hagaon Harav Dovid Feinstein, shlita

For the privilege of studying and learning under his tutelage
and the zchus of his guidance and love, which we so greatly cherish.

With profound Hakoras Hatov

Nurit and Mayer Berkovits

In special tribute to our beloved parents

Ta and Ma
And
Abba and Ima

For all that you have done and continue to do.
We do not have the words to express our deep appreciation
for your love and for your efforts to instill in us
the values which will help us build a Bayis Ne'eman B'Yisroel.
May you be zocheh to see much nachas and joy from us.

Nurit and Mayer Berkovits

Dedicated in loving memory
Of my beloved father

Reb Yitzchak Isaac ben Reb Mayer, z"l

Who, in his lifetime, imbued his family with a love of Torah and Chesed.
He was a model of an 'Ehrlicher Yid,' and this is the treasured legacy
of his children and grandchildren.

Mr. and Mrs. Yossi Berkovits

In memory of

לאה בת ר׳ מאיר ע״ה

Mrs. Lisa Schmutter

נבל״ע כ״ו ניסן תשס״ו

Together, with her distinguished husband,
she inspired her children and grandchildren
to lead lives filled with faith in Hashem,
Ahavas Yisroel, love for the Torah way of life,
and reverence for Gedolei Yisroel.
May her memory remain an inspiration

MESIVTHA TIFERETH JERUSALEM